The Woodturning Bible

The Woodturning Bible

Phil Irons

CHARTWELL
BOOKS, INC.

A QUARTO BOOK

Published in 2011 by
Chartwell Books, Inc.
A division of Book Sales, Inc.
276 Fifth Avenue, Suite 206
New York, New York 10001
USA

ISBN-13: 978-0-7858-2793-1
QUAR.WTBB

Conceived, designed, and produced by
Quarto Publishing plc
The Old Brewery, 6 Blundell Street
London N7 9BH

Project editor: Lily de Gatacre
Art editor & designer: Quadrum Solutions Pvt. Ltd.
Photographer: Ian Howes
Assistant art editor: Kate Ormes
Art director: Caroline Guest
Creative director: Moira Clinch
Publisher: Paul Carslake

Printed in China by Midas Printing International
Limited

10 9 8 7 6 5 4 3 2 1

PUBLISHER'S NOTE
Woodturning can be dangerous. Before you use
any hand or power tools, read the safety
information on pages 24–25. Always exercise
caution and read instructions carefully. As far as
the methods and techniques mentioned in this
book are concerned, all statements, information
and advice given are believed to be accurate.
However, neither the author, copyright holder,
nor the publisher can accept any legal liability for
errors or omissions.

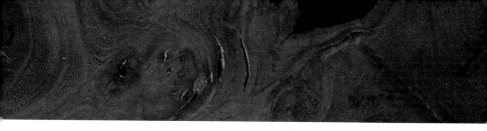

Contents

About this book

This book provides the ideal introduction for the beginner to woodturning. Basic techniques are demonstrated and followed by step-by-step projects. As your expertise and confidence grows, you will need to refer less frequently to the techniques pages and can begin to experiment.

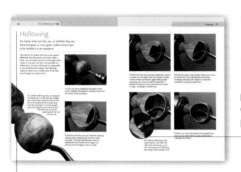

Woodturning techniques
Pages 26–71
Learn 18 fundamental woodturning skills by following the step-by-step instructions.

Enlarged details
Occasionally, enlarged details are used to explain a particular part of a process.

Numbered techniques
Techniques are numbered in the top left-hand corner so they are easy to refer to as you work on your projects.

Finishing techniques
Pages 72–97
A guide to ensuring your finished carvings are both as protected and as elegant as possible. A wide array of wood finishes are suggested with clear instructions for their application.

Professional examples
Throughout the technical sections, pieces by professional woodturners are included to show techniques in context.

Illustrated steps
Close-up details of the skills and techniques allow you to easily replicate the skills demonstrated.

Woodturning projects
Pages 98–177
This section includes 16 exciting projects for you to practice your new skills. Try adapting some of the designs used in the projects and vary the embellishments to develop your own style.

You will need
Everything you will need to complete the carving is clearly identified at the beginning of each project.

Techniques finder
This handy panel will refer you to which techniques you will need to complete this project.

Gallery
Pages 178–189
A selection of beautifully turned pieces by accomplished woodturners is included to offer ideas and inspiration.

SAFETY NOTE

For the purposes of photography, safety guards on power tools have been removed. In the workshop, always follow the manufacturer's advice. Basic safety practices can be found on pages 24–25.

Introduction

The attraction of woodturning as a hobby is that the results are almost instant: with a few basic tools and a lathe, simple items can be produced very quickly. A chunk of wood can be shaped with a chisel in a matter of minutes on a lathe, whereas with other wood-oriented crafts, such as carving, progress is much slower.

There are three distinct parts to woodturning: sharpening, turning, and finishing. To achieve good results all three have to be blended together, and equal amounts of time need to be devoted to each one. The fun part is making shavings and creating shapes, but without sharp tools you can't cut the wood cleanly to produce those shavings. And having created your shape, a well chosen and carefully applied finish will not only enhance your work, but will also protect it from the vagaries of climate and storage.

More than anything else, woodturning is one of the few manual occupations that can engage hand, head, and heart at the same time—the combination of hands-on work with the need for a keen eye, and the sheer pleasure of creating a beautiful and useful object from a blank of whirling raw material is hard to beat.

Closed form bowl (top)
Michael Jones made this bowl from a soft maple burl. It has been dyed with aniline green dye on its outer surface, and finished with a hand-polished lacquer.

Koru fern vessel (bottom)
This vessel by Gordon Pembridge was turned and carved from Macrocarpa and finished with lacquer and acrylic paints.

Choosing wood

There are thousands of different species of trees and shrubs that can be used as a source of wood. Almost all can be turned, but some are more suitable than others, some can be very unpleasant to use, and some can be a real joy.

One of the great things about woodturning is that lumber which has been discarded, overlooked, or rejected by other woodworkers is often the most suitable for turning. Branch wood, which is usually thrown away, is a very good source of material; it often costs nothing to obtain, as neighbors and friends want to get rid of it when they have trees pruned. Tree surgeons and firewood sellers are other good sources of wood. Keep your eyes open, and don't be afraid to ask. One woodturner has kept himself in free wood for many years by offering to take away cut branches.

Pick up any catalog that features blanks for woodturning, or visit a local supplier, and you will be amazed by the range, with every kind of color, grain, and figure imaginable—including the more exotic and unusual, such as spalted wood, where a fungal disease creates striking lines and colors. (Be warned that some people are violently allergic to working with spalted wood.) Each of these woods has a unique quality which, the more you work with the wood and come to know its properties, will influence your work.

Hollow forms
Sometimes color can be introduced to emphasize the natural figure of pale wood, as with two of these pieces by Phil Irons.

In the same way, some woodturners enjoy turning green or undried wood, where the moisture content has not stabilized before being worked. As the wood dries—more quickly if the walls and edges of the piece are thin, more slowly if they are left thick—uncontrolled and unexpected changes appear, thus making the design process more of a two-way exchange between the turner and the wood itself than is the case with more usual woods. Apart from the uncertainty principle, there is always the sheer pleasure to be gained from turning certain woods when wet—olive is a good example—as long, juicy shavings are sliced from the wood and the smell of the wood is almost enough to distract the turner from the task in hand.

Unusual choices
Unlikely pieces of wood can often be turned into a satisfying object. This lump of burr elm (above) looks very unpromising, but has been transformed into a beautiful hollow form (right).

Woods for turning

The samples on these pages show a small but representative selection of the finest readily available woods that are suitable for the projects in this book.

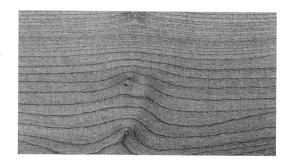

Sycamore *(Acer pseudoplatanus)*
A fine, even-textured, creamy white wood that is a joy to work and can be very decorative when rippled. A lovely wood for bowls and boxes.

Maple *(Acer)*
Depending on the species, this can be a relatively soft or fairly hard wood, with a fine, close grain that turns and finishes easily. It is usually a pale straw color, with distinctive winter and summer growth. Quilted maple is much sought after, and is very expensive.

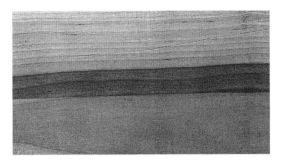

Birch (Betula)
Normally a straight-grained, even-textured, pale yellow-white wood, but if obtained from the base of the tree, birch can have a very attractive, wild, irregular grain. It is easily turned, and is ideal for hollow forms and staining.

Boxwood (Buxus sempervirens)
A very hard, close-grained, pale wood which will take fine detail—ideal for small projects such as chess-pieces, boxes, furniture knobs, etc. Because it is more of a shrub than a tree, it is only available in small sections.

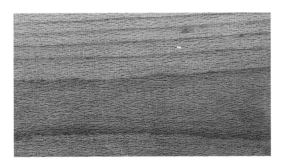

Beech (Fagus sylvatica/grandifolia)
A heavy, even-grained wood that turns and finishes easily, but is rather bland unless it is spalted (see page 10). A good wood for mallets, rolling pins, and other kitchen utensils.

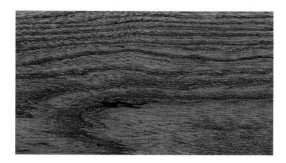

European/American ash *(Fraxinus americana)*
Although fairly coarse-grained, this wood turns and finishes quite easily. Most tool handles are made of ash, and it is good for salad bowls. Rippled and/ or olive ash is very attractive and sought after, and consequently costs more.

Plane *(Platanus acerifolia/occidentalis)*
This fine-grained, even-textured wood has an attractive fleck that is sometimes called lacewood. It works well and polishes to a fine finish; a nice wood for bowls and platters.

Cherry *(Prunus avium/serotina)*
A strong, fine-grained, even-textured wood with a very pleasant smell when worked, which turns and finishes well. It can be used for small bowls, boxes, and caddy spoons.

Oak *(Quercus)*
A massively strong wood with a coarse, straight grain. Tools need to be sharpened frequently, as it is quite abrasive. A good wood for furniture-making and spindle-turning uses, such as kitchen towel holders and mug trees.

Yew *(Taxus baccata/brevifolia)*
Europe's oldest living tree, yew is one of the most wonderful woods to turn. Although classified as a softwood, it is, in fact, quite hard. It has very distinctive creamy white sapwood and orange-red heartwood. A good wood for small turning items such as ring stands, plant forms, fungi, and so on.

Elm *(Ulmus procera/hollandica/ americana)*
Elm has a coarse, irregular grain that can make it difficult to achieve a good finish, but sharp tools can get good results, particularly if the wood is burred; this is a very attractive and very sought-after wood, good for bowls using oils as a finish.

Choosing a finish

Most objects in wood require a coating or finish of some kind, both to protect the wood and to enhance its appearance. Although you can use any type of finish on any type of wood, the choice will depend on the nature of the piece and how and where it is to be used. For details of some specific finishes and finishing techniques see pages 72–97.

Finish	Appearance	Durability	Sustainability
Wax: Beeswax is soft natural wax. Wax polish is usually a mixture of carnauba wax with beeswax or paraffin wax.	Soft shine that enhances the natural beauty of the wood.	Poor; needs regular attention if used alone. Wax polish is slightly more resilient than pure beeswax.	Best applied over another finish that seals the wood. A wax-only finish can attract dirt, so avoid it on open-grained woods.
Oil: Oil finishes include linseed, teak, Danish, and tung oils. Most wood finishing oils are based on tung oil.	Warm glow that enhances grain. Oil/varnish mixes can be applied as a high-build finish.	Fair; recoating may be necessary. An oil/varnish mix has greater durability.	Ideal for open-grained woods. Two or three coats will build up a soft sheen without obscuring the wood's tactile qualities.
Shellac: Shellac is a natural resin that can be bought as flakes that you mix with denatured alcohol, or ready-mixed.	Warm tint; beautifully lustrous when applied using French-polishing technique.	Moderate; will not withstand heat or moisture.	Makes an ideal sanding sealer before applying a wax finish. As a finish in itself, it can be low or high build (French polish).
Nitrocellulose lacquer: Fast-drying. Water-based lacquers are nonflammable, with less fumes than solvent-based ones.	Clear gloss, available as gloss, satin, or flat; water-based versions have slightly poorer color.	Good; water-based lacquers are slightly less durable than solvent-based ones.	Items that receive moderate usage and where appearance is also important.
Polyurethane varnish: Easy-to-apply synthetic resin. It gives off terrible fumes when first applied.	Clear; high-build finish can look plasticky; water-based versions can have a cold tinge.	Excellent; two-part varnishes are stronger than standard one-part varnishes.	Items that receive heavy usage.

The workshop

Where you work is a subject to which entire books have been devoted, and the various options covered range from a fully equipped professional space allotted solely to wood-working to a kitchen work surface used for turning miniature goblets, or a disused outside bathroom, with the tools hung from hooks at the back of the toilet.

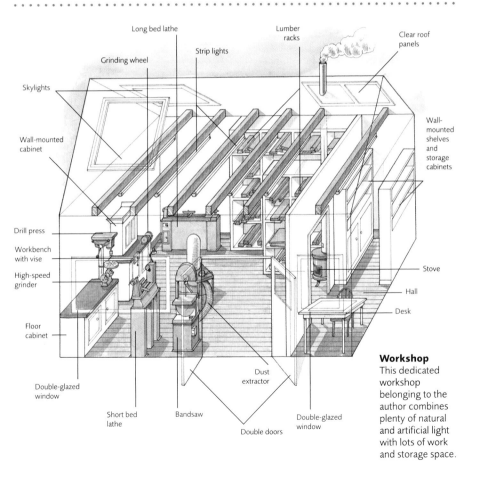

Long bed lathe

Lumber racks

Clear roof panels

Strip lights

Grinding wheel

Skylights

Wall-mounted shelves and storage cabinets

Wall-mounted cabinet

Drill press

Workbench with vise

High-speed grinder

Stove

Hall

Desk

Floor cabinet

Double-glazed window

Short bed lathe

Bandsaw

Dust extractor

Double doors

Double-glazed window

Workshop
This dedicated workshop belonging to the author combines plenty of natural and artificial light with lots of work and storage space.

For many amateur woodturners, the garage doubles as a workshop, with the lathe mounted on a bench at one end and any other equipment having to share space with the car and all the paraphernalia normally associated with a garage. This does encourage you to clean up frequently and use the space wisely, but it is hardly ideal.

- If possible, the lathe should be situated near natural light—usually a window or skylight. An adjustable lamp can be placed near or on the lathe. Make sure that the rest of the workshop space is adequately lit.

- There should be plenty of space available to move around the lathe, and to swing tool handles without any obstruction. Because the correct stance when turning is essential (see page 20), you should rethink your workshop space if you are cramped or cannot move freely.

- You can never have too many electrical outlets for stationary and other power tools, but make sure that they are installed by a qualified electrician, and never be tempted to overload sockets or power circuits.

- If you are planning to do a lot of turning, especially in adjoining living areas, some form of sound insulation should be considered.

- Woodturning in a cold environment is not only unpleasant, but can be dangerous, as your reflexes and alertness become dulled. Insulation and heat should be a priority, and if you have the space or are putting together a custom-built workshop, a shavings burner is worth thinking about; this will provide the necessary heating and will also get rid of your wood waste.

The illustration on page 17 shows one way of setting up a dedicated workshop; you can use graph paper and cut-out paper shapes to find the best way of using the space available to you. The following points should be considered, wherever you end up establishing your working space.

- Old kitchen cabinets make excellent storage spaces; some can be cut in half along their depth and be made into two.

- If you have invested in quality tools, it would be foolish to leave them lying around where they can be damaged. Make tool storage a priority. The best way to store hand tools is to hang them from pegs on walls or wall-mounted boards. Edged tools and power tools can be stored in cupboards, or on open shelving so that they are easy to see and reach.

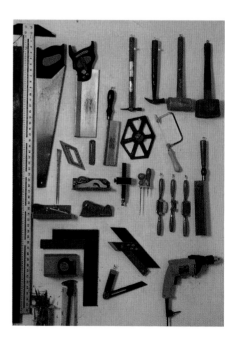

Wall-mounted storage
Some woodworkers paint an outline shadow of each tool on the board, so that they can see at a glance if one is missing.

The lathe

Before buying a lathe, test as many as possible: try out a friend's lathe, join a club or woodturning association and try all the lathes that they have, go on a course with a reputable instructor and ask for advice and opinions on the different lathes available, or visit woodworking shows to check out what's available.

Choosing a lathe

Once you have seen what there is, you have to decide just what kind of turning you want to do and how much space you have to work in—if you want to turn miniatures exclusively, you

obviously won't need a huge, floor-mounted lathe and, conversely, if you plan to make bowls and nothing else, a lathe that will only swing 6 in (150 cm) will not prove to be of any use at all.

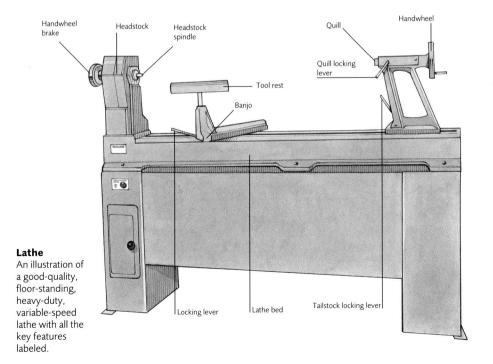

Lathe

An illustration of a good-quality, floor-standing, heavy-duty, variable-speed lathe with all the key features labeled.

Handwheel brake · Headstock · Headstock spindle · Quill · Handwheel · Quill locking lever · Tool rest · Banjo · Locking lever · Lathe bed · Tailstock locking lever

Most woodturners compromise and end up going for a swivel-head lathe that allows them to do both of these extremes and everything in between; if you decide to go this route, your lathe needs to have a good range of speeds that will cope equally with out-of-balance bowl blanks (which need a slow speed) and spindle work (which requires a high speed). A good range for this type of lathe is 300–2700 rpm, increasing in five or six steps.

When deciding whether to go for a free-standing or bench lathe, the most important things to remember are that a free-standing lathe should be as stable and as heavy as possible (so it might well not be suitable for a wooden floor without reinforcement), and that bench-mounted lathes are only as good as the bench to which they are fixed. Here, the ideal solution is to build a sturdy bench to the correct height for you—the spindle centers should be at elbow height once the lathe has been bolted securely to the bench.

As with any woodworking purchase, it is always advisable to go for the best that you can afford; here, the quality is almost invariably reflected in the price. This is not to condemn all less-expensive lathes out of hand—some are surprisingly well made and are quite suitable for learning on—but you do tend to get what you pay for.

Woodworking websites and magazines, and local newspapers often advertise secondhand lathes for sale, or you may hear of one from your local club or by word of mouth. This is certainly an excellent way to look for a lathe with a good reputation that may no longer be made, but if you are interested, make out a checklist before viewing. This should include the general condition of the lathe, and also the details—if the visible electrical wiring is in bad condition, for instance, what will the rest be like? Always ask to see the lathe running, and don't be afraid to set the different speeds or test the chuck yourself. And, if it's a free-standing model, who is going to transport it to your workshop, and is this included in the price?

Stance
How you stand at the lathe is important. The wrong stance can cause tiredness and also lead to other problems with your back and neck. When turning between centers you should stand parallel to the lathe, a comfortable distance away, with your feet about shoulder-width apart, so that as you traverse the tool you can sway your body rather than moving your feet. This is not always possible, but the tool handle should be beside your hip, rather than in front of your body. The tools should be thought of as an integral part of your body, like a pair of snow skis, which gives you greater control of the tool.

A big part of being comfortable at the lathe is its height, or the height of the centers from the floor. This should be at or slightly above elbow height when your forearm is held in a relaxed position across the front of your body. If your lathe is bench-mounted it should be fixed as close to the front edge as possible, rather than towards the middle, so that you can stand at the lathe rather than having to reach to it.

Having said all this, the main priority is to feel comfortable and relaxed, rather than be cramped or have to reach too much.

Standing at the lathe
To prevent back problems, be conscious of how you stand.

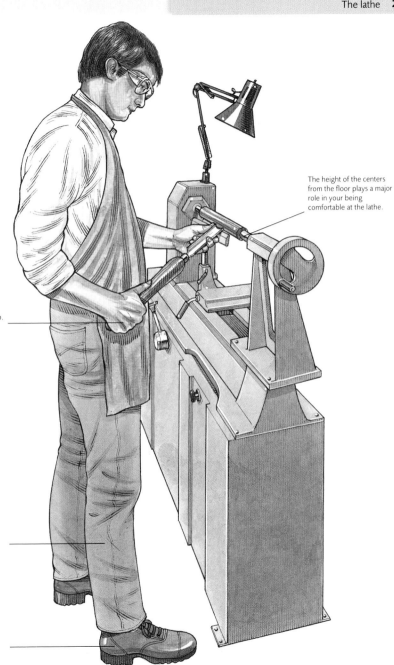

The height of the centers from the floor plays a major role in your being comfortable at the lathe.

Tool handle should be beside your hip.

Stand parallel to the lathe, a comfortable distance away.

Feet about shoulder-width apart.

Tools

There are literally hundreds of turning tools available today, and trying to select which ones to start with can be difficult. An all-round set for beginners need only consist of six tools (listed here). These will enable you to complete all the projects in this book.

STARTER KIT

Scraper (1) There are too many shapes and styles of scraper to be taken up here, but for someone just starting out, the RS 200KT multi-tip shear scraper from Robert Sorby is a very versatile tool in all sorts of applications—both cross grain and end grain—and is probably the only scraper you will need.

Bowl gouge (2) These gouges are ground out of solid round bars, and have a deep flue and a long, strong shank. They are available in sizes of $1/4$ in (6 mm), $3/8$ in (10 mm)—this is recommended for the beginner—$1/2$ in (12 mm) and $3/4$ in (19 mm).

Roughing gouge (3) This gouge is usually the first tool used in any spindle-turning application. It should only be used on spindles, never on faceplate work. Roughing gouges are commonly available in widths of $3/4$ in (19 mm)—this width is recommended for the beginner—$1^1/4$ in (32 mm) and $1^1/2$ in (38 mm).

Spindle gouge (4) There are two types of spindle gouge, one ground from a solid round bar, and the other forged from a flat strip of metal. Both types are commonly available in widths from $1/8$ in (3 mm) to $3/4$ in (19 mm), in $1/8$ in (3 mm) increments. A good starter is a $1/2$ in (12 mm) continental-type gouge.

Skew chisel (5) This can be a difficult tool to master, but with practice is also the most versatile and rewarding to use. The surface produced by a sharp skew needs little or no sanding, and can be likened to that from a hand plane. Skews come in two sections, oval and standard. Both types are available in sizes of $1/2$ in (12 mm), $3/4$ in (19 mm), 1 in (25 mm) and $1^1/4$ in (32 mm), and are ground to an angle of 30°.

Parting tool (6) A $1/8$ in (3 mm) parting tool is the next most useful item in your kit. It can be used in conjunction with measuring calipers to set sizes, create spigots for lids or chucks, and, as its name suggests, part finished pieces.

OTHER USEFUL TOOLS

Other useful tools are listed below; their uses are detailed in the appropriate sections.

Bandsaw This makes it possible to convert boards into bowl blanks and rip boards into the required sections for spindle turning.

Measuring calipers (7) These are essential for setting diameters on spindle work.

Dividers These are used to scribe lines from the centers of faceplate work, such as chuck recess sizes, and can also be used for marking out bowl blanks to be cut on the bandsaw.

Jacobs chuck Mounted on a Morse taper to suit your lathe, these can be used in either the headstock or tailstock for drilling or for holding very small pieces.

Scroll chuck This type of chuck is derived from engineers' four-jaw, self-centering chucks, and is operated by either a pair of levers or a single key. Most come with a screw-chuck adapter.

Bench grinder The standard gray wheels supplied with these grinders should be replaced with softer white wheels, to reduce heat build-up.

Wet-stone grinding system The possibility of overheating the tool's edge is totally eliminated by using this system.

Hollowing tools The brass gauge on top of the tool limits the thickness of shaving and thus prevents the tool from digging in.

Power sanding pads These neoprene pads faced with Velcro allow the quick changing of abrasive discs for easier, more effective sanding when used in an electric drill.

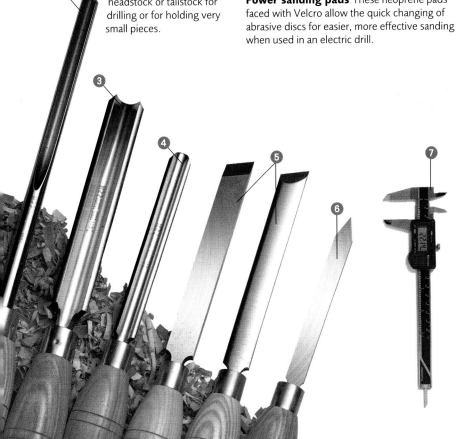

Safety

Most safety procedures are a matter of common sense, yet it's surprising how many accidents happen to people so caught up in their turning—if you'll pardon the pun—that they fail to observe the basic safety practices. Accidents can happen, whatever the precautions taken, but adhering to a few simple rules will help to prevent the most obvious ones.

- Don't wear loose clothing or neckties that could get caught in the revolving workpiece. Long hair should be tied back, and any loose or dangling jewelry removed before starting.

- It's a good idea to invest in a smock with elastic collar and cuffs to protect your clothes and prevent shavings getting down your shirt front; they usually have pockets at the back so they don't fill up with shavings.

Lighting
An adjustable lamp with a daylight bulb should be fitted to the headstock of the lathe to light the workpiece effectively.

- Wear eye and face protection, such as safety glasses, goggles, or a visor—or a filtered air visor which combines eye and face protection with respiratory protection. This draws air through a prefilter via a small fan into the main filter, and then blows clean air down the inside of the visor, which is great for glasses wearers because their glasses don't mist up.

- Before starting up the lathe, check that the spinning workpiece is not going to hit the tool rest or anything else, and make sure that the workpiece is secured and free from defects or splits that could fly off when the lathe is started.

- Switch off the lathe before making any adjustments to the tool rest, and remove the tool rest when sanding.

Goggles
Eye injuries are the most commonly reported among woodworkers, so putting on a pair of goggles or a face shield should become second nature.

- Ensure that you have enough room to move around the lathe and swing tool handles. Clean away shavings at the end of each day so that they don't build up underfoot.

- It is a good idea to wear a pair of sturdy shoes or boots in the workshop at all times; when tools fall off the lathe or bench they invariably fall edge first, and even if they don't, they can still hurt.

- Electrical safety is very important. Avoid long extension cables underfoot, regularly check all connections and electrical cords attached to your machines for signs of wear, and get them replaced by an electrician if necessary.

- Good lighting at the lathe is essential. An adjustable lamp attached to the headstock is best; it's out of the way, but can be positioned over the work without obscuring your vision, and if you have a swivel-head lathe, the lamp moves with the headstock.

- Get into a routine where you take some extra time, both before and after turning, to ensure that all the safety procedures have been followed. It should become second nature, but don't become too complacent!

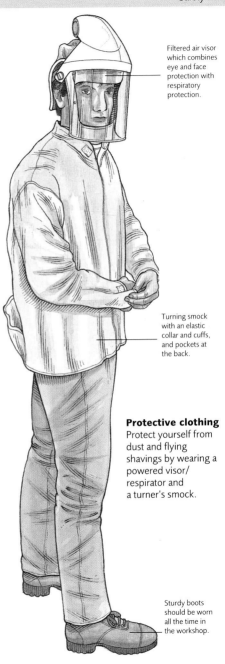

Filtered air visor which combines eye and face protection with respiratory protection.

Turning smock with an elastic collar and cuffs, and pockets at the back.

Protective clothing
Protect yourself from dust and flying shavings by wearing a powered visor/ respirator and a turner's smock.

Sturdy boots should be worn all the time in the workshop.

Hearing protectors
Wear earplugs or hearing protectors to protect your hearing from long-term damage whenever you use power and machine tools.

Techniques

Converting lumber

A chainsaw can be a very useful tool for harvesting lumber and cutting it into manageable sizes that a bandsaw can cope with. An electric chainsaw with a circuit breaker is better for occasional use than a gas-powered one, which requires regular use to remain in good condition. Chainsaws should be treated with respect, and the user should take a chainsaw safety course.

1 Here, an electric chainsaw is used to cut the end off a 14 in (355 mm) diameter x 16 in (405 mm) long beech log, to remove the splits and, reveal the sound wood.

2 You can now decide how to divide the log up to get the best from it. Using a mixture of freehand drawing and a hardboard disc, mark out the shapes and sizes of the blanks you want with a black marker pen.

3 The first cut takes a slice off the side of the log adjacent to the largest bowl blank to provide a stable base. The second cut is made down the back of the blank, stopping at the intersection of the cuts. The log is then rolled onto the flat to make the third cut, which releases that section.

4 The final cut is made to separate the large bowl from the section that contains the end-grain cylinders.

5 Use a disc of the appropriate size to mark the widths of the two bowl blanks contained in this section, then cut them in half. Repeat this process on the section containing the end-grain cylinders.

6 When cutting with the chainsaw has been completed, you can then cut the blanks more accurately on the bandsaw.

7 Pin the plywood or hardboard discs into place with an awl, and then use this as a template to cut around. These discs alleviate the problem of cutting circles from irregular-shaped lumps.

8 The discs can also speed up the cutting process when you have a flat surface to work on, as in the case of these end-grain cylinders.

9 Paint an emulsified wax sealer on the ends and $1\frac{1}{2}$ in (38 mm) down the sides of the blanks to prevent the exposed end grain from splitting until you are ready to turn them.

10 Another way to prevent blanks from drying out in the short term is to wrap them in polyethylene cling wrap, as are these blocks of sycamore that have been cut and are ready to be turned into hollow forms.

This conversion process means that you can transform unlikely-looking lumps of what would otherwise be firewood into usable turning blanks.

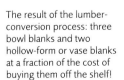

The result of the lumber-conversion process: three bowl blanks and two hollow-form or vase blanks at a fraction of the cost of buying them off the shelf!

Using a bandsaw

After the lathe, a bandsaw is the most essential and potentially the most expensive piece of equipment that you can have in the workshop, even if it is only for cutting wood to length and preparing bowl blanks.

If you are serious about turning, the savings made by preparing your own blanks over buying them pre-cut will very soon repay your investment in a decent bandsaw.

This shows the end product of about half an hour's work on the bandsaw, using timber that was destined for someone's fireplace.

1 You can easily cut small logs on a bandsaw, as long as the saw has enough depth of cut; the minimum for a bandsaw to be really useful is 6 in (150 mm), with a throat of at least twice that.

2 Hardboard discs, ranging in size from $4\frac{1}{2}$ in (115 mm) up to the maximum capacity of your lathe, are very useful for deciding how to get the most out of a log or board. The backs and drawer bottoms from old kitchen units are a good source of hardboard.

3 Pin the hardboard disc to the outside of a half log, and cutting natural-edge bowls could hardly be more simple.

Sharpening

Because they are quickly blunted by the amount of wood that they remove, turning tools need sharpening a lot more often than other hand tools. The difficulty for beginners is achieving a single-faceted bevel with the correct angle without bluing or changing the temper of the steel. Three different techniques are shown here, ranging from the simple and inexpensive to using a professional-quality machine.

Lathe-mounted sharpening

The beauty of this system is that your line of sight is parallel with the face of the disc, which makes it very easy to line up the bevel. Modern turning tools are produced with a flat bevel rather than concave, because manufacturers grind the bevels on flat belts.

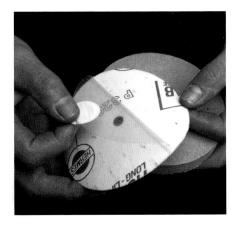

Basic technique

1 The simplest system can be made in your own workshop or bought as an inexpensive kit. It consists of two $^3/_8$ in (10 mm) thick x $5^1/_2$ in (140 mm) diameter MDF discs with self-adhesive abrasive discs in three different grits (80, 150, and 320) and a leather disc, which are mounted on a central screw or directly onto your screw chuck.

2 You can make an arbor that fits the jaws of your chuck to facilitate quick changing of the discs, without tying up your screw chuck. This will also ensure that the discs always run true if you should make the face slightly concave.

3 Stick the leather on one face of a disc, using contact adhesive, and the 320 grit on the other; these are the faces that will be used most often. Just before screwing it onto the arbor, run some thin superglue into the hole to create a more permanent thread.

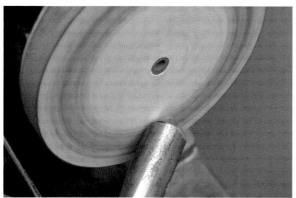

4 Position the tool rest at 90° to the disc and as low as possible. Lay the tool to be sharpened—here, a ³/₄ in (19 mm) roughing gouge—on the rest at an angle so that the bevel is parallel to the face. Try to use the bottom of the disc so that the direction of rotation is away from you. Set the lathe on a medium speed.

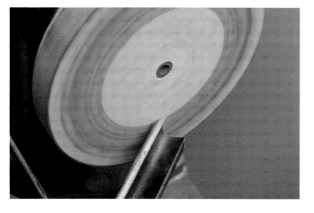

5 Keeping the angle of the tool the same, slowly rotate it to sharpen the whole face of the bevel. Light, even pressure is all that is needed to keep the bevel in contact with the abrasive.

Sharpening skew chisels

Skew chisels are one of the trickiest tools to sharpen: where the face must be ground concave, a lot of metal has to be removed to achieve a single facet. The discs make it easier—simply line up one flat face to another, then turn the tool over to do the other side.

Sharpening parting tools

To keep parting tools square across the end, maintain them horizontally on the tool rest at the correct angle.

Radiusing skews

Both oval and standard-section skews can be radiused easily by putting up the bevel at the correct angle and rolling the handle slightly away from the perpendicular to produce a radius.

Honing
1 You can produce an even keener edge and polished bevel on finishing tools like the skew and spindle gouge by honing them on the leather disc. The surface of the leather is loaded with a honing compound, which will remove the burr thrown up by the abrasive and polish the bevel.

2 Honing should always be done away from the edge and the bevel kept flat against the leather. As tools lose their edge they can be honed several times before needing to be reground.

Macadamia wood bowl
Bob Stocksdale is a master of the classic bowl form. By choosing the right wood and carefully aligning the grain orientation, he has painted a sunburst in wood.

Bench grinding

High-speed bench grinders are designed to remove material very quickly, but this can cause several problems. Far more metal is removed than is actually necessary to keep a tool sharp, and as turning tools need sharpening regularly they can have a very short lifespan.

Again, because metal is removed very rapidly, a lot of heat is generated, especially at the edge, where it is thin and most sensitive to heat. Carbon-steel tools need to be quenched in water regularly to prevent them getting too hot and turning blue, which destroys the temper or wear resistance, and means the tool will no longer hold an edge. The tool then has to be reground back to good steel, without overheating again. However, high-speed steel (HSS) tools are not affected in the same way—the bluing only affects the look of the tool—but they must not be quenched, as HSS contracts very quickly, causing fine cracks which could fracture.

Some of these problems can be overcome by using grinding jigs, which when set correctly allow you to pass the tool quickly over the wheel before too much heat is generated; if the tool does need to be quenched, it is put to the wheel at exactly the same angle, which produces a single facet every time.

Safety note—Eye protection should always be worn when using a bench grinder.

1 Most jigs of this type have an adjustable arm with a cup at the end mounted directly under the grinding wheel. With the tool handle in the cup, adjust the arm in or out until the tool rests on the wheel at the correct angle.

2 So that the previously ground angle is duplicated and more of the tool is not ground unnecessarily, you can use a simple method of checking. Color part of the bevel with a permanent marker.

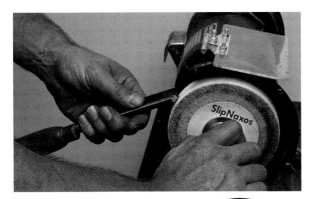

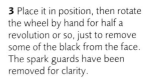

3 Place it in position, then rotate the wheel by hand for half a revolution or so, just to remove some of the black from the face. The spark guards have been removed for clarity.

4 If the black mark is missing from the heel, the arm needs to come out a bit, and vice versa.

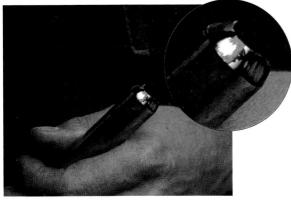

5 Once the correct angle has been attained, roll the tool quickly from edge to edge across the face of the wheel to sharpen it. All square-edge tools, such as parting tools and carpentry chisels, can be ground like this, but without the rolling action.

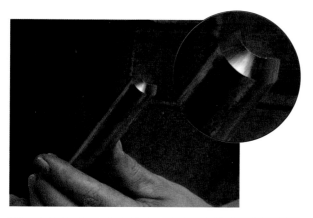

6 This is what a well-ground bevel should look like: one single facet from edge to edge.

Maintenance
Bench grinders are usually sold with general-purpose gray wheels which are hard, glaze quickly, and generate a lot of heat. These should be changed for softer white or pink wheels which generate far less heat. All grinding wheels need to be dressed with a dressing stick, star wheel dresser, or diamond dresser to expose a fresh cutting surface on the wheel and to maintain squareness.

Sharpening gouges
1 Grinding jigs are essential for sharpening swept-back bowl gouges, where the tool is not just ground across the end, but down the sides of the tool as well. The shank is clamped into the jig and the leg of the jig pivots in the cup, allowing the tool to pass through a wide arc.

2 The length the tool protrudes out of the jig and the distance of the arm cup govern the grinding angle, and are simply reproduced by marking the arm with different lengths for different gouges. You can measure the tool protrusion by pushing it up to a preset stop on the bench as the tool is clamped into the jig.

3 Spindle gouges manufactured from round bars need a "ladyfinger" profile, which is difficult to grind freehand. Because they have a very fine angle, the jig for them has a different angle and a longer leg to produce the necessary profile.

Wet-stone grinding

Although wet-stone grinding is quite slow, it eliminates the risk of overheating the tool, while the slow-running wheels are made of fine material, which in turn produces a far superior edge than any other form of grinding. The various jigs available give you total control over whatever tool you are sharpening.

Skew chisels

1 Skew chisels are difficult tools to sharpen without overheating or changing the bevel angle. On the wet-stone grinder the large diameter of the wheel and the slow speed, combined with the simple jig, make the task a fairly easy one.

2 You can hone the bevel to remove the burr raised by the grinding, and polish the bevel to give an even finer edge.

3 An adjustable gouge jig allows you to produce the compound bevels required for swept-back bowl gouges repeatedly and with ease.

Spindle gouges
1 Spindle gouges can be ground exactly to your favorite profile with the same jig.

2 You can then power-hone the gouge at the same angle on the leather strop.

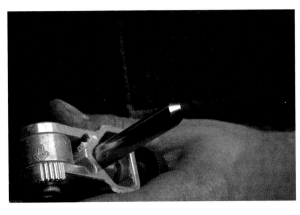

3 The polished bevel is the same as that used by carvers to get a fine finish directly from the tool, without any need to sand.

Honing

A cutting edge is usually honed with a slipstone or fine diamond lap to remove the burr produced by grinding, but sometimes it works the other way around. Scrapers, especially shear scrapers, need a burr to work, as the burr produces the fine shavings. Rather than repeatedly grinding to produce a rather coarse burr, a very fine burr can be formed by honing.

1 Remove any remains of the old burr by rubbing the lap or slipstone over the top of the scraper.

2 Push the lap once or twice along the edge to raise a fine burr.

3 The resulting burr produces fine shavings and a surface from the shear scraper that requires less sanding.

Center finding

Finding and marking accurate centers for turning blanks is vital to good woodturning for several reasons. The first, and probably the most important, is that it means that the blank is properly balanced, and therefore is less likely to fly off the lathe; and the second is that if a square section is included in the design of the turned piece, it must be central to the axis.

Finding the center with a ruler
There are all sorts of gadgets to find the centers of turning blanks, but the simplest method is to lay a straightedge or ruler from corner to corner and draw a pencil line, and do the same from the opposite corners on both ends of the blank. Where the lines intersect, make a small indentation with an awl.

Using a center-finder
1 This commercially available center-finder has a knife edge that accurately marks the center. To use it, position the blank and tap it with a mallet, then turn it through 90° and tap it again.

2 If you have a lot of pieces in which you need to find the center, this gadget speeds things up and can even be used on cylinders, for which it is normally troublesome to find the center.

Mounting between centers

Turning between centers means that the workpiece is held between two points, a drive center which grips the wood, and a tail center which supports and provides enough pressure for the drive center to grip. Basically there are three types of drive center: two-prong, four-prong, and friction drives, available in a variety of sizes.

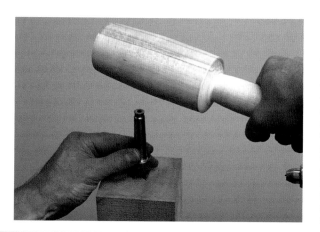

Pronged drives
Two- and four-prong drives need to be driven into the wood for the drive dogs to locate firmly. Having found the centers, stand the blank on a solid surface, locate the point on the center mark, and give it several sharp taps with a wooden mallet; this should be enough to locate the drive dogs. Insert the center into the Morse taper of the headstock before relocating the blank onto the drive dogs.

Friction drives
You do not need to drive a friction-drive center into the workpiece in the same manner as a pronged drive; instead, locate the point in the awl mark in the center of the blank.

Mounting the blank

1 When the blank has been located on the drive center, slide the tailstock into position so that the tail center is just short of the blank, then locate the tail center in the other awl mark by winding the tailstock handle. With a pronged drive, apply pressure with the tailstock to ensure that there is no movement between the drive dogs and the wood. Using a friction/ring drive, you can vary the amount of pressure the ring has seated by backing the hand wheel off a bit.

2 When the blank has been successfully mounted, position the tool rest parallel to the workpiece and about level with the height of the centers. The workpiece must be rotated by hand to check that it clears the rest by at least $^1/_4$ in (6 mm).

3 Before turning on the lathe, check that everything is securely in position and won't move during turning.

Mounting on a screw chuck

Bowl blanks can be mounted in a variety of ways: screwed directly to a faceplate, glued to a waste block which is then screwed to a faceplate, a faceplate ring screwed to the blank, then fixed onto the chuck, and so on. One of the simplest and quickest methods is to use a screw center or screw chuck to hold the blank while the outside of the bowl is turned.

1 Screw centers and chucks come in various sizes and lengths. If the screw center is too long for a shallow bowl, a spacing washer can be made to reduce its length. With modern deep-grooved, parallel-thread screws, a 2–3 in- (50–75 mm-) thick bowl blank only needs about 1 in (25 mm) of screw thread to hold. The face of the washer needs to be slightly concave to allow for the fibers that pull out around the thread.

2 A recommended hole size is usually supplied with the chuck. Mark the required depth of hole on the drill bit with a piece of tape, and make sure that the hole is at right angles to the face of the blank.

3 Screw the blank firmly onto the chuck until the faces of the washer and blank meet squarely.

Chuck mounting: expansion

There are two ways of holding a bowl to hollow out the inside: a recess into which the chuck jaws expand or a spigot that the jaws grip. Both of them need to be cut accurately for maximum grip and stability. This sequence demonstrates the first method.

1 The optimum grip of a chuck is achieved when the jaws are slightly opened to form a complete circle; this is the point at which the whole rim of each jaw is in contact with the recess.

2 Transfer this measurement with the dividers to the underside of the blank, being careful not to let the outer come into contact with the upward rotation of the blank.

3 Cut the dovetail out to the scribed line with the long point of a skew chisel. The depth of the recess for a bowl of this size need not be more than $1/4$ in (6 mm).

4 As long as it doesn't interfere with the seating of the jaws, the recess can be decorated with small beads to disguise it. Before locating the recess onto the jaws, check that it is clean, with no dust or shavings that might impair the positioning of the jaws.

Roughing

The roughing gouge is primarily used to rough out a blank; that is, to take it from square section to round when working between centers.

In any spindle-turning application, the roughing gouge is normally the first tool used and should only be used on spindles, never on faceplate work. Roughing gouges have a wide, deep U-shaped flute with a fairly thick wall section; they are usually ground square across the end at an angle of about 45°. For the beginner, a $^3/_4$ in (19 mm) width is recommended; other commonly available widths are $1^1/_4$ in (32 mm) and $1^1/_2$ in (38 mm).

Basic technique
1 If the workpiece is longer than the tool rest, position the rest so that the gouge can't fall off it before the cut is finished; it should be parallel to the work and about center height. To get used to the movement, do a dry run first: put the gouge on the rest about 2 in (50 mm) from the end of the blank, with the handle held low down beside your body. Roll the flute over slightly and point the gouge in the direction of the cut, i.e., toward the tailstock. Keeping the gouge on the tool rest, raise the handle and at the same time slide the tool along the rest towards the tailstock.

2 Check that the workpiece rotates freely and everything is locked up tight, then start the lathe and begin the movement again. Gently raise the handle until you hear a knocking sound, which is the heel of the bevel touching the corners of the blank. Raise the handle until the gouge starts to cut and shavings appear, then traverse it along the rest at the same angle; keep the shavings flowing until the gouge is clear of the rotating wood, then push the handle down again.

3 Repeat the process described in step 2, and continue making the cuts until you have a cylindrical surface with no flat area on it. Start each cut a little further towards the headstock, and when you reach about 2 in (50 mm) from that end, stop cutting.

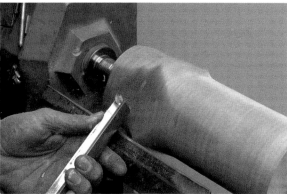

4 When you reach this point you must reverse the direction of the cuts. It is safer to cut away from the end of the workpiece than to cut into it, as there is less chance of the tool digging in. Practice roughing out a cylinder on a number of pieces—they won't go to waste, as just about everything you make between centers needs to be roughed out first.

Planing cuts
You can also use a roughing gouge to make planing cuts. Here, the flute faces slightly toward the workpiece, instead of away from it, and the angle at which the gouge is presented to the wood is much greater, so that a slicing cut is made. This should produce a nearly polished surface.

Parting

In addition to their primary function—that of parting finished items from their waste blocks—parting tools can be used to perform a variety of other tasks.

There are six types of parting tool, all of which are useful in their own right: **standard-section**, available in $^1/_8$ in (3 mm) or $^1/_4$ in (6 mm) widths—the $^1/_8$ in (3 mm) type is the most suitable for a beginner; **diamond-section**, which is $^5/_{32}$ in (5 mm) wide at the center or waste line; **fluted**, $^5/_{32}$ in (5 mm) wide at the flute, which runs down the underside of the tool; **beading and parting**, which has a $^3/_8$ in- (10 mm-) wide square section; **bedan**, which has a single bevel and is rhombus-shaped in a $^3/_8$ in- (10 mm-) wide section; and **super-thin**, which is $^3/_{32}$ in (2 mm) thick.

Bevel rubbing

The standard, parallel-shanked parting tool should nearly always be used with the bevel rubbing and be held at right angles to the workpiece. Start the cut with the heel of the bevel rubbing, then gently raise the handle vertically until you reach the desired depth of cut. To remove the tool from the cut, lower the handle.

Making sizing cuts

1 To make sizing cuts, the parting tool is used in conjunction with a set of Vernier calipers or adjustable measuring calipers.

2 When you use calipers, you will obviously have to hold the parting tool one-handed. Hold it at the top of the handle, with your index finger extended up the blade and the lower part of the handle resting under your wrist.

Box-making
Super-thin parting tools are used where the least possible amount of wood is to be removed, such as in box-making, where a good grain match between the lid and body is needed.

Parting off
Sometimes it is easier to use a parting tool one-handed in your left hand, gripping it in exactly the same way as with the right, while the right hand cups the item that is being parted off.

Cutting dovetail spigots
You can use the parting tool, as seen here, to cut a dovetail spigot that matches the one of the jaws of the scroll chuck.

Using a spindle gouge

There are two types of spindle gouge: one is ground from a solid round bar, and the other is forged from a flat strip of metal.

The ground type has an uneven wall thickness due to its method of manufacture, and needs to be ground with a fingernail profile with an angle of about 40° to compensate for this. The forged, or continental, type has an even wall thickness throughout its section, and is usually ground with a slightly radiused profile at the cutting edge, with an angle of about 45°. Although they are more expensive, these gouges are worth buying, because they are easier to use. In the main, spindle gouges are used to cut coves and hollows, but in experienced hands can be used to produce a wide range of shapes on spindles.

Spindle gouges are commonly available in widths from $\frac{1}{8}$ in (3 mm) to $\frac{3}{4}$ in (19 mm), in increments of $\frac{1}{8}$ in (3 mm); a $\frac{1}{2}$ in (12 mm) continental type is recommended as a starter tool. They come in such a variety of sizes because a gouge will not easily cut a cove less than its own width.

Cutting coves
1 Coves are produced by making scooping cuts to either side of a hollow. The edge is unsupported when starting a cut, so lay the tool on its side, with the handle down and the flute facing the center of the intended hollow. Raise the handle and start the cut with the tip of the cutting edge; once the bevel has support, roll the gouge as the cut progresses, until the bottom of the hollow is reached.

2 As the cut reaches the bottom of the hollow, the flute should be almost flat. Push the handle down to bring the edge away from the wood.

3 Continue the procedure, cutting either side until you have the width of cove that you require.

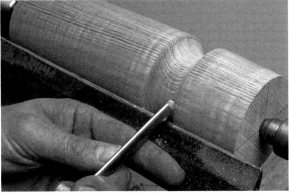

4 With the workpiece shown stationary, you can see how the gouge is presented to start the cut.

5 The gouge should finish, as shown, in the bottom of the hollow as it rolls out of the cut.

Cutting beads
1 You can cut beads with a spindle gouge. Hold the gouge at right angles to the workpiece with the bevel rubbing, then gently raise the handle and roll the tool over onto its side at the same time.

2 The tool should finish in the position shown, with the flute facing away from the bead.

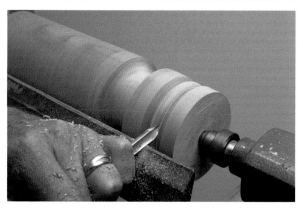

3 Do the cutting with the right-hand half of the edge, and finish up cutting at the tip of the edge as the handle is lifted and rolled into the base of the bead.

4 To cut the other side of the bead, follow the same sequence of cuts. As an exercise, try cutting a series of coves and beads along a length of scrap practice wood.

Honey dippers
Palmer Sharpless originally designed these honey dippers to be used with his daughter's ceramic honey pots. But, having turned more than 9,000 of them, he has made them his trademark, and he now uses them to teach and demonstrate turning.

Using a skew chisel

The skew chisel is to turners what the hand plane is to cabinetmakers: it should produce fine shavings and a smooth, clean surface that needs little or no finishing.

Although it is one of the more difficult tools for the beginner to use, once mastered it is efficient and rewarding. For descriptive purposes, the cutting edge of a skew is divided into three sections: the long point or toe, the center, and the heel or short point. If the back of a skew is referred to, it means the edge of the blade that forms the long point.

Skews come in two sections, oval and standard. The oval skew has no sharp corners to it that can catch in any nicks on the tool rest, and slides smoothly along the rest. It has a thinner section than a standard skew and is fine for small, delicate work. For general turning, a standard $\frac{3}{4}$ in (19 mm) skew is more suitable for beginners. Both types are available in sizes of $\frac{1}{2}$ in (12 mm), $\frac{3}{4}$ in (19 mm), 1 in (25 mm), and $1\frac{1}{4}$ in (32 mm), and are ground to an angle of 30°.

Planing cuts
1 The most basic cut made with the skew is a planing cut, where you want a smooth, flat surface. Present the chisel to the workpiece at an angle of about 45°, with the tool rest slightly above center. With the bevel rubbing, cuts are made with the center section of the edge as you move the chisel along the tool rest.

2 If you allow the tool to roll and the cutting edge moves toward the long point, a dig-in will occur as the unsupported point of the skew is forced into the wood by the rotation.

3 If you let the cut move to the heel, the chisel will skid off in the opposite direction to which the cut is being made, causing an unintentional spiral.

4 When you make a planing cut from left to right toward the end of the workpiece, the shavings will be produced from the center section of the cutting edge.

Cutting "V" grooves
1 The long point, or toe, is used when cutting "V" grooves. Lay the tool on its back at 90°, so that the long point is nearest the work. Hold the handle low while lining up the tool.

2 Gently raise the handle to make the initial cut; this will not be very deep, but enough to establish the center of the groove. Any more, and the sides of the toe will start to bind.

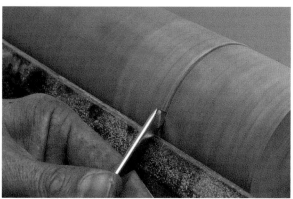

3 Exactly the same procedure is used to widen the groove, except that you present the tool at the angle required for the sides of the groove. Line up the chisel at the appropriate angle with the handle held low, and then gently raise it to make the cut.

4 Alternate these cuts on either side until the required depth and width of groove are achieved. These can be made very small, as decoration, or deeper and wider, to serve a function, such as the foot massager (see pages 118–120).

Radiused cutting edges

1 The heel, or short point, is used to radius the sides of the "V" grooves to create beads. This is a slightly more complex operation, as you need to raise the tool handle, roll it, and sweep it around all in one motion, while keeping the bevel in contact all the time.

Radiused edge

Conventional

2 The standard-section skew shown on the left has been ground to produce a radiused cutting edge, as opposed to the one on the right, which has a conventionally ground profile.

3 The benefits of a radiused cutting edge are that when making planing cuts the heel and toe are further away from the surface, thus reducing the chance of them catching and digging in, and making the tool a bit more user-friendly.

Using a bowl gouge

Bowl gouges are supplied ground square across the end, so you need to grind back the wings so that they don't catch.

The compound angles that are now being used on swept-back gouges, commonly known as the "Irish grind," overcome this problem with a steep bevel angle at the point; as the bevel sweeps around to the wings, this angle becomes a lot more acute. On the outside of a bowl these gouges are drawn across the face, rather than being pushed, as with a conventionally ground gouge; on the inside of a bowl they are used in much the same way as the standard grind. The problem here for a beginner is that a lot of practice or costly jigs are required to replicate the grind each time the tool needs sharpening.

Depending on the amount of bowl turning you do, you will probably need more than one gouge, ground at different angles to cope with different depths and shapes. Bowl gouges are ground out of solid round bar, with a deep flute and a long, strong shank, to cope with the distance by which they sometimes have to overhang the tool rest. They are available in sizes of $^1/_4$ in (6 mm), $^3/_8$ in (10 mm), $^1/_2$ in (12 mm), and $^3/_4$ in (19 mm); $^3/_8$ in (10 mm) is recommended for beginners.

1 When using a bowl gouge, it is more important for the bevel to rub than when using a gouge between centers. If possible the handle should be held down by your hip, and any movement of the tool should be made with your body.

2 Keep the tool rest as close to the work as possible to minimize the amount of tool overhanging the rest. This does, however, make it difficult to effect a single cut from the base to the rim to finish off.

Using a scraper

On the whole, scrapers are a rather inefficient way of removing a lot of material when working on cross-grain work, such as bowls, and between centers, i.e., spindles.

However, they can also be very effective when hollowing end grain or working with very hard, dense hardwoods as long as the lathe speed is high and the edge is kept sharp. For the beginner, the RS 200KT Multi-tip shear scraper from Robert Sorby is a very versatile tool in all sorts of applications, and is probably the only scraper you will need.

When working cross grain, scrapers should only be used to produce the best possible finish with a tool before sanding begins. Shear-scraping, or shear-cutting as it should be called, is where the tool is presented to the face at an angle of about 45°, creating a slicing action which cuts very cleanly and is a lot safer than conventional scraping.

1 Use a narrow, dome-ended scraper with the tool rest positioned above center, making sweeping cuts from the center outwards.

2 The best way to refine the interior shape is to make a light cut by pulling the tool toward you from the base to the lip, following the profile.

Drilling on the lathe

There are two main ways of drilling on the lathe.

In the first, the drill is fixed in a Jacobs chuck on a Morse taper mounted in the rotating head-stock spindle, and the workpiece is advanced onto the drill. This method is used in projects that require drilling before they are turned, such as tool handles. In the second, the workpiece is held in a chuck and the Jacobs chuck is mounted in the tailstock, which is advanced into the workpiece. The sequence below shows the second technique.

1 Find and mark the centers of your blank with an awl. Fix the drill bit into the chuck, and the chuck into the lathe spindle. Place the blank between the drill and tail center, locating the drill in the hole made by the awl. At this stage apply only enough pressure with the tailstock to hold the blank in place. Position the tool rest so that one face of the blank just rests on it.

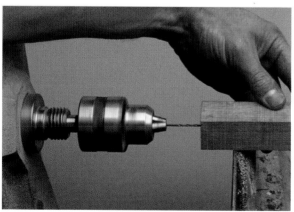

2 Steady the workpiece with one hand before switching the lathe on with the other, then advance the tailstock until you have achieved the required depth.

3 Flat-bottomed, saw-toothed bits are the best type to use in this type of drilling operation; the lathe speed should be relatively slow when using them, about 500 rpm.

4 Slide the tailstock up and lock it into position, then steadily advance the drill into the revolving workpiece until it reaches the marked depth. Clear the shavings by backing the drill out frequently before they pack up around the shank and make it difficult to remove the drill.

Rolling pin
The right choice of wood—in this case, birch plywood, walnut, and rosewood—combined with artistic vision can turn something functional like a rolling pin into a piece of usable art, like this rolling pin by Rude Osolnik.

Coning

Turning bowls can sometimes be quite wasteful, especially deep bowls or ones made from highly figured and expensive wood. There are several ways to save the centers of bowls and thus be able to make use of what would normally end up as scrap on the workshop floor.

The sequence shown here demonstrates how to use a slicing tool which cuts cone-shape pieces from the center of the bowl. This is ideal for shallow or deep bowls—the only problem is that the wood saved is always cone-shaped. The safest way to use a slicing tool is to work from the headstock side of the bowl, breaking the bowl away from the cone, rather than trying to break the cone out of the bowl, which risks damaging the spigot or recess.

1 With the bowl blank mounted on a screw chuck or small faceplate, turn and finish the outside with either a recess or spigot for mounting on the chuck. The tool rest is positioned just above center height to allow the slicer to cut with a slight scraper action; that is, with the tip pointing downward.

2 The cut has to be wide enough to prevent the tool from binding on the sides as the cut progresses to the required depth—three-and-a-half widths of the cutting edge is usually sufficient for a cut 7–9 in (178–230 mm) deep. The tool should be advanced no more than $^3/_8$ in (10 mm) at a time before moving to the cut next to it, and so on.

3 The point at which the bowl can be broken off depends on the size of the bowl and the strength of the wood; in the example here, the breaking-off point was $1\frac{1}{4}$ in (32 mm) wide. To break the bowl away, align the grain perpendicular to the lathe bed and pull with one hand, while giving the top of the bowl a sharp blow with the other, which should break it free.

4 You can either turn the outside of the next bowl now and repeat the process to create a series of bowls, or you can save the cone for a later project. Mount the outer bowl on the spigot prepared earlier, and turn and finish the inside as you would normally.

Here, the largest bowl is 16 in (405 mm) in diameter and 6 in (150 mm) deep; what would usually become shavings has been saved to make another bowl 11 in (280 mm) in diameter and $3\frac{1}{2}$ in (90 mm) deep.

The remaining cone, 7 in (178 mm) in diameter and $2\frac{3}{4}$ in (70 mm) deep, was saved for a later project.

Nesting bowls

Another way of saving wood is to cut multiple bowls with a bowl-nesting device. This has curved blades mounted on a swiveling platform, and cuts several hemispherical bowls from one blank.

• •

A bowl-nesting device is suited to bowl blanks with thicknesses of $3^1/_2$–7 in (90–178 mm), and will remove centers ranging in diameter from 4–12 in (100–305 mm). It is ideal for the production of sets of bowls, such as salad bowls and serving dishes, or nests of decorative, natural-edge bowls.

In this example, a 10 x 4 in (255 x 100 mm) blank produced three bowls: the largest 10 x 4 in (255 x 100 mm), the middle size $7^1/_2$ x $2^1/_2$ in (190 x 65 mm), and the smallest $5^1/_2$ x $1^3/_4$ in (140 x 45 mm).

1 Here, the outside of a 10 x 4 in (255 x 100 mm) blank is turned and mounted on the chuck. The platform is then mounted on the tool rest, with the cutter tip at center height, and attached to the tailstock for stability. It is then positioned and secured in place to cut the required size.

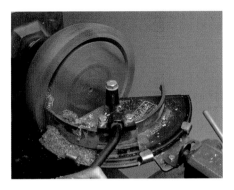

2 Pull the handle around in a controlled movement so that the cutter is slowly fed into the spinning blank as it follows the preset arc.

3 When the cut has been completed, put the center to one side and turn and finish the bowl normally.

4 Turn and finish the back of the saved center, and mount it back on the chuck ready for its center to be cut out with the smaller blade.

The finished bowls form a matching set, cut from a single blank.

Hollowing

No matter what size they are, or whether they are done end grain or cross grain, hollow forms have to be tackled in a set sequence.

The interior of a hollow form has to be treated differently than the interior of a bowl. With a bowl, cuts are made from the rim through to the center in one pass, but this is not possible in a hollow form, as most of the time it is impossible to see what the tool is doing. The following sequence allows you to keep track of the tool even though you cannot see it.

1 Once you have established the shape of the vessel, establish the depth by drilling a hole down the center of the workpiece.

2 Cranked hollowing tools are designed so that the tip is in line with the straight part of the shank, and thus the tool rest has to be positioned far enough away from the opening for only the straight part of the shank to sit on the tool rest. The hand acts as a pivot, gripping both the tool and the rest.

3 Deal first with the area just inside the opening, making small sweeping cuts from the center outwards. The final wall thickness must be established and finished at this stage, as it will become too fragile to return to later.

4 When the neck area has been dealt with, remove a central core of waste in the next section to allow room to maneuver the tool, again making small sweeping cuts. Clear the debris frequently; if allowed to build up, it can cause the tool to grab or dig in, resulting in a broken pot.

5 Finish the walls in each section before you move on to the next. The wall thickness should be constantly checked with calipers to avoid the possibility of going through them.

6 Continue hollowing in the same manner, and when the sides start narrowing in, pull the cuts toward you, following the sweep of the outside curve.

7 When you reach the bottom of the depth hole, clean up any marks left by a saw-toothed bit to complete the interior.

Finishing techniques

Sanding

Sanding should be thought of as an integral part of turning rather than an afterthought, but it should not be used as an extra shaping technique—it should be used only after the best possible finish has been achieved from the turning tool.

Begin sanding with a grit low enough to remove any imperfections left by the tooling; this will depend on the wood. Fine, straight-grain woods need less sanding than irregular or figured woods, where it can be difficult to finish with the tool without leaving some torn grain.

It is worth investing in good-quality cloth-backed abrasives, as they last longer and often have an anti-clogging coating—120, 150, 180, 240, and 320 grits should cover most of your needs, but sometimes you may need to use a coarser or finer grit. The first grit used removes the imperfections left by the tools, then the following grits remove the marks left by the preceding grits, until you have a scratch-free surface. Just using 120 and then 320 grits will not give you a good finish—the grits in between have to be used as well.

Sanding by hand is mostly confined to spindles, where it should be kept to a minimum so as not to lose crispness of detail. The tool rest should be removed in the interests of safety.

Self-powered sanders are available in two types, one using standard paper or cloth, Velcro-backed abrasive on a neoprene arbor, and the other using a Velcro/neoprene/abrasive sandwich of sanding pads on a stiff arbor with an indexed head, which is handy when trying to sand in areas where it is not possible to reach with a drill.

Hand sanding
For safety, hold the strips of abrasive underneath the spindle. The dust travels away from you toward the extractor pipe, and, if you lose grip of the abrasive, it also flies away from you, rather than toward you.

Cloth-backed abrasives
From left to right: 100, 120, 150, 180, 240, 320, 400, and 600 grit cloth-backed abrasives, and their corresponding effects.

Self-powered sanding
1 The sanders are powered by pressing one side or the other against the rotating wood, which then spins the arbor and causes it to sand.

2 Although a little slower than sanding with an electric drill, self-powered sanders are far less bulky and noisy, and are more maneuverable.

3 Running your hand over the surface while the workpiece is stationary gives you an idea of how things are progressing.

Drill-powered sanding

An electric drill can provide the motive power to speed up the sanding process; it can also be used to remove stubborn areas of torn grain and to sand pieces with irregular openings or natural edges while the workpiece is stationary. Although power sanding is more efficient, you still need to use the recommended grades of abrasive in order to achieve a scratch-free surface.

Electric drill
Variable-speed drills offer the most versatility. Start at a low speed and increase the speed to suit your needs.

1 Here, a 3 in (75 mm) arbor is used on the inside of a bowl in the sanding zone, the section between the "2 o'clock" and "4 o'clock" positions. The upper edge of the pad is in contact with the surface, rotating in a clockwise direction, while the bowl rotates in a counter-clockwise direction. The most efficient way to sand the inside of a bowl is to start in the center and work toward the outer edge.

2 When power sanding the outside of a bowl, present the arbor to the surface at an angle so that the outer portion of it is trailing; this reduces the risk of the leading edge of the pad catching or being pulled under the workpiece.

Sanding while stationary

1 Because of the very uneven outline of this natural-edge burr platter, it would be dangerous to try sanding it while it is spinning. Apart from the safety aspect, the crispness of the natural edge is preserved by sanding the piece while it is stationary.

2 When you have invested a lot of time in creating a work of art, such as this large hollow form, it would be a shame to spoil its integrity with sloppy finishing.

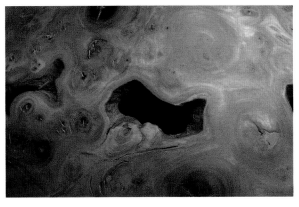

3 The attraction of a piece such as this is the detail, and if those details are blurred, part of that attraction is lost. It's worth spending a little extra time sanding around the openings with the piece stationary, rather than sanding over them while it is spinning.

4 When turning wet or green timber, such as this sycamore vase, a hair-drier or hot-air gun can be used to dry the surface enough to prevent the abrasive from becoming clogged.

5 Always try to position the dust-extractor hose as close as possible to the workpiece without obstructing your access.

6 Delicate rims such as this need to be sanded by hand, rather than taking the risk of damaging or breaking the piece by using the power sander.

Detail sanding

Brushes for detail sanding are similar to wire brushes, but have nylon bristles that are impregnated with different grades of abrasive. They are ideal for finishing textured or uneven surfaces without destroying the detail.

Here, a detail sander is used to sand the textured surface of a small bowl. With the bowl stationary, one area is done at a time so that the bristles rotate along the striations, rather than across them; the bowl is then rotated by hand to the next area.

Detail sanders are ideal for removing any debris from irregular and inaccessible areas, such as these bark inclusions, before the surface surrounding them is sanded. Because of the direction of rotation, each area is sanded one way, then the drill is set in reverse and the area is sanded again in the other.

SANDING HINTS AND TIPS

You can cut up abrasive sheets with scissors or by folding and tearing. One recommended technique is to cut sheets into quarters. Do not simply fold sheets in four, because the abrasive coats will then be facing each other and are likely to wear more quickly. Use a block, made of cork, wood, or rubber when sanding flat surfaces. Maintain an even pressure when sanding by hand. Convex or concave blocks (as appropriate) make sanding curved surfaces easier and more efficient. If the abrasive is too sharp, take off the first edge by rubbing it on scrap wood or metal. Tap abrasive paper on the back when it becomes clogged with dust. Check the surface of the wood frequently by using an oblique light source to show up imperfections. Use fingers to check the finish—they are often better than eyes.

Making feet

All bowls have a foot of some description, whether it is the spigot used to hold the bowl in the chuck or something more elaborate.

The foot or feet of a bowl can emphasize its shape and form by raising it off and separating it from the surface it sits on. Here are two different ways of creating feet: the first involves quite a lot of hand work, and the second, by contrast, is a lot simpler.

Cut-out feet

The diameter and depth of the bowl you are turning will always dictate the size of the foot, and accordingly the size of the jaws used. The feet need not be as big as those shown here, but they can totally change the aesthetics of the bowl to which they are applied.

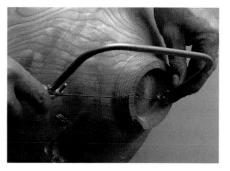

1 The spigot on this bowl has been turned so that it is long enough—1 in (25 mm)—to create three feet that will be in proportion with the rest of the bowl and have a span wide enough to support it. The recess in the center must be of a depth to follow the curvature of the bowl when the waste is cut away. Most lathes have some form of dividing head which can be used to mark out equally the positions of the feet.

2 Decide the shape and size of the feet that fit the bowl, and cut a template out of card. Center the template on the previously made mark and pencil in the outline of each foot.

3 Using a fretsaw, carefully cut away the waste between each foot. Sight the saw blade through an imaginary point at the center of the recess so that the cut faces are all aligned to the center.

4 Remove any excess waste left by the saw and refine the spaces between the feet with a rasp. You can now see why it was important for the recess to follow the curve of the bowl.

5 Starting with a coarse, 80-grit abrasive and a small-diameter arbor, blend the cut-away sections into the surrounding surfaces so that there are no blemishes, and until the surfaces flow together.

6 Using progressively finer grades of abrasive, sand these areas to the same finish as the rest of the bowl.

The feet of the finished bowl form a seamless part of the the design.

Turned feet

The technique of attaching turned feet lends itself well to shallow, natural-edge bowls or platters turned from relatively thin slices of burr; because of their irregular shape, the feet need not be equally spaced, as with the previous example. The bowl shown in this section is a slice of Australian York gum burr that measures 14 in (355 mm) at its widest point and is 1½ in (38 mm) thick.

1 The back of the bowl has been turned to a very shallow curve and the chuck recess cut and decorated. To determine the position of the feet, rotate the bowl by hand while holding a pencil on the tool rest to create an imaginary circle so that the feet are all the same distance from the center. Make a mark on the tool rest. Space the actual positions around this line.

2 Once the positions have been finalized, drill the holes with a ¼ in (6 mm) bit to about the same depth into which the feet will be glued later.

3 Turn the feet to a simple design, using a suitably strong, fine-grained wood that complements the bowl—boxwood was used here. If the design of the feet is too complicated, they can look contrived.

4 The flange at the base of the dowel should be slightly undercut so that just the rim sits up tight to the underside of the bowl, rather than there being a gap. Turn and finish the upper face of the bowl before finally gluing the feet into place.

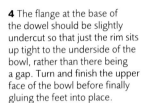

5 Sand the bottoms of the feet parallel to the surface on which the bowl will stand.

Carving

Some of the easiest woods to work, such as European sycamore, silver birch and basswood, are very bland, and are often overlooked in favor of more colorful or figured woods. Objects made from these woods can sometimes look stark, even when they have good form and proportion. Their appearance and tactile qualities can be greatly enhanced with some form of surface embellishment; sometimes large surface areas can be broken up with a few simple grooves or may need something more elaborate. Examples of two different methods are shown in this section.

Carved decoration—for example a band of flutes around the neck of a vessel—breaks up the visual line of a piece, and can draw attention to an otherwise stark form. The carving does not need to be very deep to be effective; in fact, just enough for the light to catch on the irregular facets.

Using a power carver
1 Tools you would not normally associate with turning can be used to create some wonderful effects. The texturing on this hollow form, which looks as though it was laboriously chip-carved, took just a few minutes to produce.

2 An angle-grinder-mounted, power-carving blade is passed across the surface of the slowly rotating workpiece to achieve the texture required.

3 The tool should be presented so that the direction of the blade's rotation cuts with the grain. Cut from the largest diameter to the smallest.

4 By changing the angle of the grinder, the resulting pattern appears to spiral around the workpiece; this is a bit trickier than working horizontally.

Carving by hand
1 A band of strategically placed carving can really enhance an otherwise bland form. Here, a raised band is decorated by hand with shallow carved flutes; the same effect can be produced using a power carver and will be considerably faster.

2 The tool rest is used to guide the carving tool, with the workpiece rotated by hand before the start of each cut. The height of the tool rest above, at, or below the center line governs the direction or angle of the cuts.

3 Here, a herringbone pattern is produced by making a series of cuts with a V-gouge with the rest below center height, and then the same number of cuts made with the rest above the center line.

Scorching

Burning the surface of a bowl that you have spent some time turning might seem a bit drastic, but it can be a very effective means of decoration.

Open-grained or coarse-grained wood, like oak, ash, or sweet chestnut, is more suitable for scorching than fine, close-grained wood, and burrs take on a crumbled appearance.

1 In scorching, the surface of the object is burned with a blowtorch to blacken it and give it an aged and weathered appearance. This type of decoration does not lend itself to thin-walled bowls and the like, which would probably burst into flames.

2 When the surface is burned quite dark, the softer summer growth, burning away quicker than the winter growth, leaves a layer of soot that is removed with a fine wire brush to reveal the true surface.

3 Sometimes you can cut a series of grooves to define certain features—in this piece, the band below the rim.

4 You can leave parts of the object natural. Here, the chuck recess was left because the accuracy could be affected by the scorching, it provides a nice contrast, and leaves you somewhere to sign, date, and identify the wood.

Scorching is only really suitable for coarse, open-grained woods, such as oak, where there is a distinct difference between the summer and winter growths.

Texturing and coloring

As well as being a very tactile material—there is always something about it that makes you want to touch it—wood can also be decorated in ways that immediately involve and attract another of our senses—sight.

· ·

The small, rippled ash bowl in this example combines both texture and color to gain our attention.

1 The upper surface of this bowl has been turned to a slight convex shape with a bowl gouge and is then shear-cut to remove any ridges or undulations.

2 The lathe is set to run at a slow speed, about 300 rpm, and a powered mini-carver is drawn across the face to create the surface texture.

3 The result is a slightly spiraled, indented surface. Similar results can be achieved by vigorously brushing along the grain with a stiff, hand-held wire brush, which scours out the softer areas of the grain and leaves the harder areas, giving the surface a weathered appearance.

4 To accentuate the natural ripple, two different colored stains are applied. A dark purple stain is first brushed on over the entire area.

5 To encourage maximum penetration, a second coat of purple is applied after the first has dried. Note how the ripple is highlighted by the color.

6 To smooth the raised and slightly torn grain without reducing the textured effect, a medium-grade detail sander is used in an electric drill. This also removes any excess stain lying on the surface.

7 In this example, the second color applied is orange, which is brushed over the whole surface and allowed to dry.

8 The fine-grade detail sander is used to remove any raised grain and excess stain. It also gives the surface a final polish.

9 The slightly undercut hemispherical hollow is cut with a $1/4$ in (6 mm) bowl gouge and then sanded smooth; be careful not to round over the crisp rim.

10 Several coats of an acrylic metallic varnish are applied to the interior of the hollow. The tangerine color is a vivid contrast with the rim, but at the same time complements it.

11 The ragged edge caused by the mini-carver is cut back to an even, flat chamfer with a gouge and carefully sanded to a finish.

12 A black permanent marker is used on this narrow chamfer to mask the seepage of the stain. It also acts as a border, somewhat like a picture frame.

13 Several coats of clear cellulose lacquer are sprayed onto the piece before it is waxed and polished.

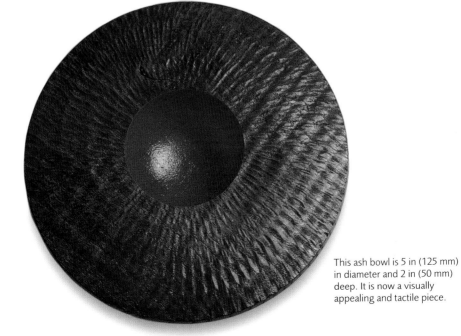

This ash bowl is 5 in (125 mm) in diameter and 2 in (50 mm) deep. It is now a visually appealing and tactile piece.

Grooving

Decoration can take many forms, and the simplest can often be the most effective. In this example, a sharpened hacksaw blade mounted in a wooden handle is used to create a series of evenly spaced grooves on the underside of a bowl.

1 The surface to be grooved is finished, apart from the last two grades of abrasive, 240 and 320 grit. The wooden handle acts as a depth limiter so that all the grooves are of an equal depth, and the tool rest is set at a height to ensure that the blade cuts on the center line. On a concave surface like this, present the tool to the surface at right angles all the time, so that the ribs retain as much strength as possible. The spacing of the grooves is done by eye. When the whole area to be grooved has been finished, the final sanding can be completed in preparation for the finish—oils are recommended for this type of decoration.

The grooving is framed by the two plain bands at the top and the bottom of the bowl, relieving an otherwise fairly stark profile.

Finishes

The type of finish should be appropriate for the use of the article. For example, items that are to come into contact with foods or to be used by small children need a non-toxic finish; liquid paraffin is ideal because it is non-toxic, colorless, and does not go rancid. Try out different finishes until you find what suits you—but remember that no finish can cover up hasty surface preparation.

Friction polishing
Friction polish should only be used for small decorative items, because it can be quite difficult to achieve an even finish on larger surfaces.

1 With the lathe stationary, wipe or brush on an even coat of polish, making sure to get it into any corners.

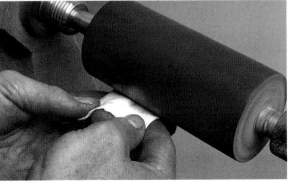

2 Start the lathe and gradually build up pressure with the towel until you have the desired luster, without streaks or lines. If the finish is too shiny, apply a coat of wax with 0000-grade steel wool to soften it.

Oiling

Most woodfinishing oils are based on tung oil, a natural oil that penetrates the wood. They also contain resins and driers to give heat- and water-resistance, and the dry surface will not scratch or chip. Two or three coats are needed to build up a nice soft sheen without obscuring the wood's tactile qualities, and the workpiece can be easily recoated at a later date if necessary.

1 The easiest way to apply oils is with a brush. Apply a liberal coating to the whole object and leave it to soak in for a time; the actual time will vary according to the manufacturer's recommendations and the weather conditions.

2 After the appropriate time, wipe off any excess oil with kitchen towel. For the best results, leave the item to dry overnight, then lightly rub it with 0000-grade steel wool to remove any dust particles that dried with the oil, and reapply the oil.

Oiling is an ideal finish for open-grain timbers and items with natural apertures, where it would be difficult to apply other types of finish.

Applying liquid paraffin

This is a non-toxic finish readily available from drugstores and is ideal for use on anything that will come into contact with children or food.

1 Sand the workpiece normally, running through the different grits until you reach the final grit, then brush on a coat of liquid paraffin over the whole surface. Do this with the lathe stopped, otherwise you may end up covered in the finish yourself.

2 Restart the lathe and use your final grit—320 or 400 grit—to sand the liquid paraffin into the surface. One of the benefits of using this method is that it reduces the amount of dust that you have to cope with; another is that the item can be easily maintained.

This hardwood spatula was sanded and finished with liquid paraffin for a non-toxic, food-safe result.

Spraying

Any spraying should always be done in a well-ventilated area kept as dust-free as possible. Clear automotive lacquer dries very quickly and gives a very durable finish for decorative items. It can be built up to give highly figured woods a deep, lustrous effect.

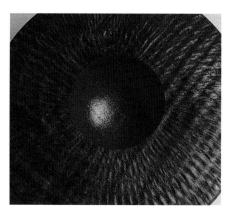

1 A Lazy Susan bearing screwed to the underside of a wooden disc makes an excellent turntable for placing items to be sprayed, as they can be rotated without being touched and spoiling the effect.

2 Applying several light coats will give a better finish than one heavy coat.

Fence-post bowl

This bowl started life as a fence post in outback Australia, where it stood for many years. Jarrah is impervious to woodboring insects and Jules Tattersall has used the aged wood to great effect, exploring the contrast between the weathered exterior and the pristine nature of the wood beneath the surface.

Waxing

To reduce the harshness of a highly glossed finish, it is best to apply paste waxes with 0000-grade steel wool.

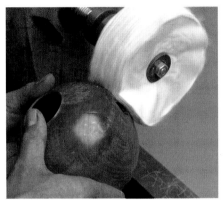

1 Take up a small amount of wax on a pad of 0000-grade steel wool, and use light pressure and a circular motion to apply the wax evenly.

2 Once the wax has dried, it can be polished off by hand or, less laboriously, on a slow-running buffing wheel that is reserved for the purpose.

Saturn box

Made from one piece of burr boxwood, this box, by Hans Weissflog, shows what can be achieved when technical mastery and patience are combined. The outer disk is loose but is held in place by the box.

Projects

Design principles

The whole question of designing in wood is far too extensive to be gone into in any great depth here, but there are a few pointers that are worth considering, apart from the highly subjective aspects of dimensions and proportions.

· ·

The first thing to consider is, what is the purpose of the piece—purely functional, purely decorative, or somewhere in the vast expanse between these two poles? In between, being the largest category, has the most possibilities and opportunities for design, but the largest number of possible pit-falls: it is no good coming up with an elaborate shape for a salt shaker, for example, if you then cannot use it to pour salt efficiently. As with most parts of the woodturning process, there is no substitute for trial and error; and don't forget to keep a record of the design process and the technical side—happy accidents always occur, and can be a major part of the learning curve.

Bear in mind also that design must take into account the context in which the finished piece will be kept or displayed. If you are planning to turn a large bowl, do you have a particular place where it can be shown to best advantage? A quick look around any museum, craft fair, or exhibition will show both the pros and cons of positioning and context.

Designing a set
Creating a unified set of pieces brings its own demands and requirements. In this coral series, Nick Arnull uses the same pattern to unify the set while the colors and shapes of the pieces vary.

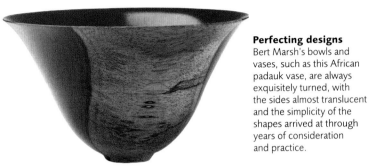

Perfecting designs

Bert Marsh's bowls and vases, such as this African padauk vase, are always exquisitely turned, with the sides almost translucent and the simplicity of the shapes arrived at through years of consideration and practice.

Functionality and design

A standard-shape rolling pin is a perfect example of a design where simplicity is arrived at through function—if the pin does not work properly and is not comfortable to use, no amount of decoration will make it any good.

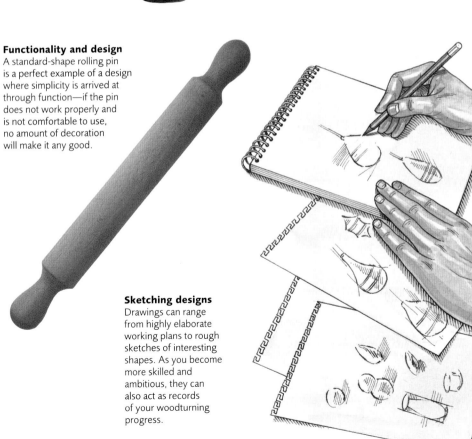

Sketching designs

Drawings can range from highly elaborate working plans to rough sketches of interesting shapes. As you become more skilled and ambitious, they can also act as records of your woodturning progress.

Spindle turning

The term "spindle turning" means that the workpiece is fixed between the centers of the lathe and the grain is running parallel to its axis. Cutting is always made downhill—or to put it another way, cuts are made from the largest diameter to the smallest, cutting with the grain rather than against it.

• •

By far the best tool for spindle work is the skew chisel. Although initially more difficult to master than the gouge, it is the most rewarding of tools to use. The only way to master the skew is to practice with it, and the projects in this section are designed to include use of the skew.

For beginners the words "skew chisel" and "dig-in" are often synonymous, with the tool seemingly determined to damage or destroy the workpiece with a large unplanned spiral. If this happens you are probably gripping the tool too tightly, giving the point nowhere to go but deeper into the wood. If your knuckles are white when you use a skew, you need to loosen up. Another way of improving your technique is to use a skew with a curved cutting edge; while you are making planing cuts the long and short points of the edge are further away from the wood, thus reducing the chance of catching.

Mallet
With practice, you can use a skew chisel and the spindle-turning method to create numerous pieces.

Spindle-turning ideas
1 Rolling pin
2 Spatula
3 Mallet
4 & **5** Door wedges
6 Cord pull
7 Rattle
8 Foot massager
9 Tool handle
10 Garden dibber
11 Cereal stirrer

Cord pull

In this simple project you can make a cord pull out of almost any wood or to match other wooden bathroom fittings. The pull is a simple teardrop shape with a screw-in eye in the end, to which the cord can be tied.

· ·

TECHNIQUES FINDER
5: Center finding, page 45
6: Mounting between centers, pages 46–47
9: Roughing, pages 50–51
12: Using a skew chisel, pages 58–61

1 Find and mark the center of your blank (Technique 5). Mount the blank between centers and adjust the tool rest (Technique 6). Rotate the workpiece by hand to make sure that it is not going to hit the tool rest, then switch on the lathe and use the roughing gouge to turn the blank down to a cylinder (Technique 9).

2 Using a pencil, scribe a line $^3/_8$ in (10 mm) from each end; these are the waste areas that double as a safety zone so that you don't accidentally hit the drive and tail centers with your tools and damage both.

3 Starting at the tailstock end of the blank, use the parting tool to cut a groove to a diameter of $^3/_8$–$^1/_2$ in (10–12 mm) on the tailstock side of the line. Make this a clearance cut so that the tool doesn't bind, and then repeat at the headstock end of the blank, making the cut on the headstock side of the line.

4 Using either the skew chisel (Technique 12) or spindle gouge, round off the headstock end with small cuts, moving the tool from right to left. Make the finishing cut meet the bottom of the groove cut earlier with the parting tool. The start of the curve—at its largest diameter—should finish about a third of the way along the length of the pull.

5 Move to the other end of the blank and make the same cuts, this time moving the tool from left to right. Start the cuts at the tailstock end and move the tool in the same arc as the finished shape. Watch the profile as you make the cut—this will give you a good idea of what is happening to the shape. With practice you will be able to adjust the cut just from looking at the profile.

6 Stop the lathe occasionally and look at the overall shape and proportions of the piece, and also check the surface to see what your cutting is like. Aim for a nice, full curve from one end to the other, without any flat spots.

7 As well as being decorative, evenly spaced grooves or "V" cuts at the largest diameter also serve as a grip. Before cutting, mark where you want the grooves with a pencil, then cut shallow grooves on the pencil lines about $^1/_{16}$–$^1/_8$ in (2–3 mm) deep with the long point of the skew.

8 It is a good idea to leave the stubs or waste at either end of the workpiece fairly thick while the majority of the turning is done, in case a "dig-in" occurs, which could snap them off. They can now be reduced to $^1/_8$–$^3/_{16}$ in (3–5 mm) with either the spindle gouge or skew.

9 Sand the workpiece. This may seem tedious, but it is just as, if not more, important than the turning. With a cord pull it is vital to get as good a finish as possible, because it is going to be seen and felt every time the light is turned on.

10 Although a friction polish produces a high-gloss shine with only one coat, it is not very durable, especially in a moist bathroom. Brush on several coats of Danish oil for a durable finish (see page 94).

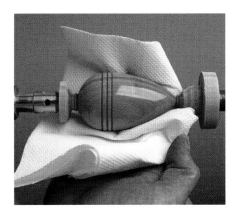

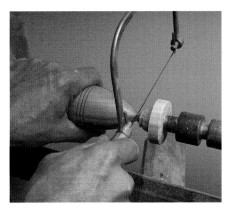

11 When applying any finish with the lathe running, be careful if using rags or cloth, as loose threads can be caught in the rotating wood, sometimes with disastrous results. The safest thing to use is paper towel, which will disintegrate before causing problems.

12 To remove the stubs, use a coping saw or any fine-toothed saw. Don't do this with the lathe running. After cutting off the tailstock stub you will have to remove the piece from the lathe anyway.

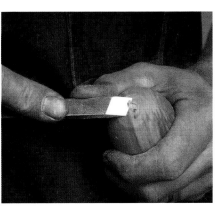

Once you have screwed in the eyelet and attached the appropriate cord, your cord pull is ready to use.

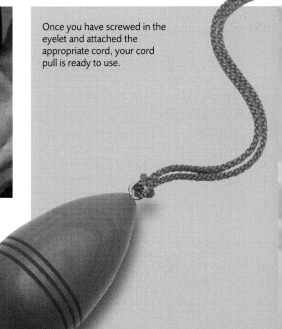

13 Use a sharp knife or skew chisel to clean up the ends, and lightly hand-sand the area (see pages 74–79). Apply your chosen finish, and you have completed your first turning project!

Rolling pin

Rolling pins come in all kinds of shapes and sizes. In this project you will make one without handles, but it can be easily adapted to have handles (see steps 16 and 17). This is an exercise in controlling the skew chisel in order to achieve a variety of cuts, mainly planing but also rolling half a bead.

• •

TECHNIQUES FINDER	**5:** Center finding, page 45	**11:** Using a spindle gouge, pages 54–57
	6: Mounting between centers, pages 46–47	**12:** Using a skew chisel, pages 58–61
	9: Roughing, pages 50–51	
	10: Parting, pages 52–53	

1 Find and mark the center of your blank (Technique 5). Mount the blank between centers (Technique 6) and adjust the tool rest to the desired height and distance from the workpiece. Rotate the workpiece by hand to make sure that it is not going to hit the tool rest, then switch on the lathe and use the roughing gouge to turn the blank down to a cylinder (Technique 9).

2 Set the calipers to a diameter slightly less than the one you have achieved with the roughing gouge—in this case 1$\frac{7}{8}$ in (47 mm). Holding the parting tool in one hand and the calipers in the other, cut a groove about $\frac{3}{8}$ in (10 mm) from one end until the calipers will just pass over the flats in the bottom of the groove (Technique 10).

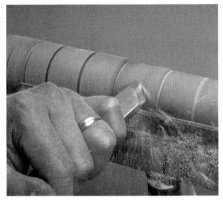

3 Continue the whole way along the cylinder at intervals of about 1¹/₂–1³/₄ in (35–40 mm). The diameters of these grooves should all be identical; if not, reset the calipers to the smallest diameter and carefully recut the others to create points of reference that will make it easier to turn a perfect cylinder.

4 Using your skew "long point" up, make planing cuts to reduce the areas between the grooves (Technique 12). Blend each cut into the previous one until there are no steps, but don't remove the parting tool marks. As you move the tool through each cut, watch the profile to see how much material you are taking off; note how the shavings are coming off the middle of the tool.

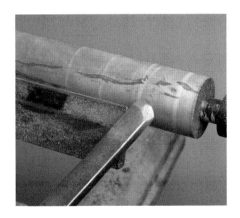

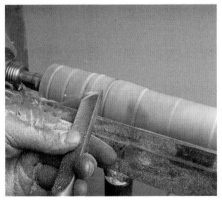

5 When you are concentrating hard on a tool like the skew, it is very easy to forget where it is on the tool rest and run off one end, which can be disastrous to both the project and yourself. Be careful!

6 When you are about three-quarters of the way along, move the tool rest to the other end and make cuts in the other direction. The reason for this is that the bevel is supported by the wood as you run off the end of the workpiece. Some other time, start a cut with any tool without bevel support, and you will see why.

7 Continue the sequence of cuts until you reach the section that you cut in the other direction, again making sure that you don't take out the parting tool marks. The cylinder should look parallel now, without undulations or high spots.

8 Color one edge of the straightedge with the crayon and put it against the workpiece with the lathe running. The crayon will rub off onto the high spots. You can make a straightedge from a piece of hardwood planed true, ideally slightly longer than the workpiece.

9 Take some very fine cuts to remove the crayon marks, then recolor the straightedge and put it on again to check; if necessary, take some more fine cuts until you are happy with the results. By now the parting tool marks should have disappeared as well.

10 Using the parting tool, make a cut at either end just wide enough to cover the penetration of the tail and drive centers; usually one width of the parting tool is enough. Make sure to stop the cuts just short of the centers—if you are using a single-point tail center, leave a bit extra for safety.

11 Radius both ends of the pin with the skew as though you were cutting one half of a bead. Remember to start with small cuts and roll the skew around the curve, keeping the cut in the middle of the face all through the cut.

12 When you have a smooth radius, reduce the spigots at either end with the long point of the skew. Remember to lean the cutting edge slightly away from the face you are cutting to avoid digging it in. Leave enough material to be able to sand safely, but not so much as to make paring away the stub a chore.

13 You shouldn't need to do much sanding after using the skew. The easiest way to sand long spindles is to use the whole width of the abrasive sheet, holding each end of the sheet and moving it from one end of the workpiece to the other (see pages 74–79).

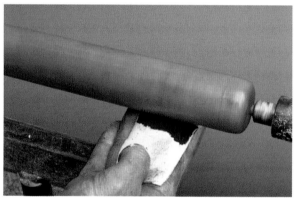

14 Any wooden utensil in contact with food needs to have a safe, non-toxic finish. Pharmaceutical liquid paraffin is available in small quantities from druggists, and in larger quantities from veterinary suppliers. Sand it into the wood with your final grade of abrasive, here 320 grit.

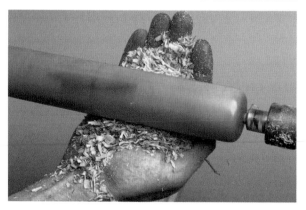

15 Hold a handful of shavings against the slowly rotating workpiece to clean off the excess oil, and polish the surface at the same time.

16 This project can easily be adapted to be a pin with handles by starting with a longer 6 in (150 mm) blank. Mark 2 $^{3}/_{4}$ in (70 mm) for each handle with a pencil, leaving $^{3}/_{16}$ in (5 mm) for the waste stub. Use the measuring calipers and parting tool to set the smallest and largest diameters of the handle.

17 The aim here is to make both ends look the same, so don't try too difficult a shape; keep it nice and simple. Shape the handles with the spindle gouge, remembering to cut from the largest to smallest diameters all the time (Technique 11), then sand and finish as described in steps 13–15.

The finished rolling pin will need to be re-oiled from time to time.

Tool handle

Turning tools can be expensive. However, many
are available without handles, and one way to
reduce the cost is to make your own, or you may
need to replace an old handle. This project shows
you how to make a basic handle which may be
a copy of one that you own.
• •

TECHNIQUES
FINDER

5: Center finding, page 45
10: Parting, pages 52–53
12: Using a skew chisel, pages 58–61

1 Steady the blank with your hand and switch on
the lathe. Don't try to drill the hole all at once, but
back off the blank to clear the debris from the drill;
you may need to do this two or three times to
reach the required depth. Remove the drill chuck
and replace the drive center (Technique 5).

2 Measure the internal diameter and length of
the ferrule or length of copper pipe—here, a ³/₄ in
(19 mm) diameter ferrule was used.

3 Next, mount the blank between the centers, locating the tail center point into the drilled hole, and rough out the blank. Mark the ferrule length and cut the diameter up to the pencil line with the parting tool and Vernier calipers (Technique 10).

4 Stop the lathe and trial-fit the ferrule; it should be a snug fit that just needs to be tapped into place, not forced. If the spigot is too large, replace the blank between centers and trim to fit the ferrule.

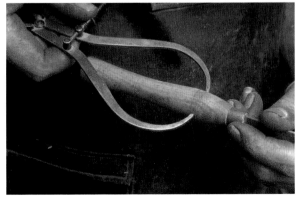

5 Using the calipers, size the tool handle that you want to copy at the largest and smallest diameters, and transfer them to the blank.

6 Use the calipers and parting tool to cut the large and small diameters on the blank.

7 Starting from the tailstock end, shape the handle using the skew chisel (Technique 12); be careful not to cut the ferrule spigot.

8 Work your way toward the headstock, copying the original handle.

9 You can decorate the handle with a series of small "V" grooves or use thin wire to burn in some lines (see pages 86–87). Sand the handle but not the spigot area (see pages 74–79).

10 Polish the handle with friction polish or Danish oil (see page 94). Remember always to use paper towels when applying any finish to a rotating workpiece.

This particular handle was made for a homemade captive ring tool.

Foot massager

This foot massager consists of three beads—the one in the middle is shallower than the other two and has a series of "V" grooves cut into it. It is a good exercise in skew-chisel control, where an off-the-tool finish is all that is needed because the massager is rolled on the floor under a bare or stockinged foot to relieve aches and pains at the end of a hard day at the lathe.

· ·

TECHNIQUES FINDER	
6: Mounting between centers, pages 46–47	**12:** Using a skew chisel, pages 58–61
9: Roughing, pages 50–51	
10: Parting, pages 52–53	
11: Using a spindle gouge, pages 54–57	

1 Mount the blank between centers (Technique 6) and use the roughing gouge to turn the blank down to a cylinder (Technique 9). Cut the waste spigots at both ends, and mark the center and length of the beads to 1$^1/_8$–1$^3/_8$ in (30–35 mm).

2 Set the calipers to 1$^3/_8$ in (35 mm) and cut a groove with the parting tool inside both lines (Technique 10).

3 Use the spindle gouge to create the beads at either end of the workpiece (Technique 11).

4 Cut the bead in the middle with either the skew chisel or spindle gouge, leaving the pencil line and tapering down to the base of the end beads.

5 Using a pencil or the point of the skew chisel, divide the section equally on either side of the center line to create the centers of each "V" groove— here, there were six.

6 Cut the "V" grooves to an even width and depth, on both sides of the center line, using the long point of the skew chisel (Technique 12).

7 Clean up the beads, and if necessary take any sharp ridges off the tops of the grooves. When you are satisfied, reduce the waste stubs and part off with the parting tool.

8 Hand-sand the ends to remove any whiskers or torn grain.

Rattle

Captive rings have intrigued people for centuries, and are a way for turners to show off their skills. Whether used singly, as decoration on the stem of a goblet, or a number together between a couple of beads to make a rattle, this technique is quite easy and very satisfying, and always impresses people. Try using unseasoned wood—in small sections, it will dry slightly oval without cracking, and create more intrigue.

· ·

YOU WILL NEED

FOR TURNING
• Roughing gouge
• Parting tool
• Skew chisel
• Spindle gouge
• Ring-cutting tool
• Fruit wood, i.e., apple, cherry, plum, etc.; dimensions 1¹/₄ x 1¹/₄ x 5¹/₂ in (30 x 30 x 140 mm)
• Top speed of your lathe

FOR FINISHING
• Liquid paraffin or other non-toxic finish

TECHNIQUES FINDER	**6:** Mounting between centers, pages 46–47	**12:** Using a skew chisel, pages 58–61
	9: Roughing, pages 50–51	
	10: Parting, pages 52–53	
	11: Using a spindle gouge, pages 54–57	

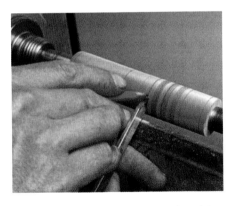

1 Mount the blank between centers, and rough it out to a cylinder (Techniques 6 and 9). Pencil in the waste spigots, measure ³/₄ in (19 mm) from this line, and mark. From the tailstock end, use the width of your parting tool and pencil-mark nine lines and then another line ³/₄ in (19 mm) from the last line.

2 To avoid mistakes, shade in the areas that will be the rings. The ³/₄ in (19 mm) areas are the beads, which you can mark with a center line if you wish.

3 Make cuts on either side of the beads and in the unshaded areas to a depth of approximately ¹/₄ in (6 mm), using the parting tool (Technique 10).

4 Create the beads and tops of the rings with the skew chisel (Technique 12). You may find it easier to cut one side of all of them and then the other.

5 Try to make all the beads and rings even without any flat spots. This technique is a good test of your control of the skew chisel.

6 To work the handle, use the spindle gouge to cut a shallow cove which tapers from the headstock end toward the first bead (Technique 11).

7 Sand and oil the whole workpiece at this stage, before you start to cut the rings.

8 Use a ring-cutting tool to undercut the rings, working them all from one side and then from the other until they break free.

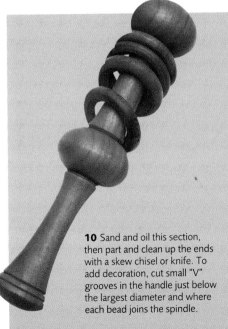

9 Clean up the spindle underneath the rings with the spindle gouge, creating another shallow cove. Make sure that the rings can freely touch the beads, otherwise the rattle will be less effective.

10 Sand and oil this section, then part and clean up the ends with a skew chisel or knife. To add decoration, cut small "V" grooves in the handle just below the largest diameter and where each bead joins the spindle.

Mallet/tenderizer

A wooden mallet is a useful thing to have around the workshop, especially for a woodturner. Using a metal hammer to locate drive centers will eventually bell the ends so that they don't fit into or damage the Morse taper. This project creates a mallet with a slightly domed face and a convex end, which is adapted to make a meat tenderizer with a flat face with deep "V" grooves cut into it.

TECHNIQUES FINDER	**5:** Center finding, page 45 **6:** Mounting between centers, pages 46–47 **9:** Roughing, pages 50–51 **10:** Parting, pages 52–53 **12:** Using a skew chisel, pages 58–61

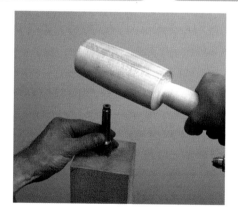

1 Find the centers on your selected blank and mark them with pencil lines (Technique 5). Stand the blank on end on a solid surface—the lathe bed or the corner of your workbench—line up the drive center and give several sharp taps with a mallet to locate the drive dogs firmly.

2 Place the drive center in the lathe spindle. Locate the drive center in the previously made marks, bring up the tailstock and lock it into position (Technique 6). Wind the tail center in just enough to secure the blank safely.

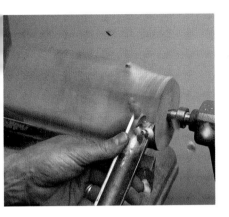

3 Start at one end, using the roughing gouge to make cuts with a scooping motion (Technique 9). Work toward the headstock, continuing this sequence of cuts until you are almost at the end.

4 Change direction for the last few cuts, so that you are working from right to left. You should have a smooth cylinder at this stage.

5 Using the parting tool, cut down each end to create the waste spigots (Technique 10). Measure 6 in (150 mm) from the headstock end and mark with a pencil line; this is the handle section, which can be reduced quite dramatically by taking large shavings.

6 Continue to develop the handle, taking less dramatic cuts, until you are somewhere near the right diameter.

7 Cut the underside of the head as cleanly as possible at a fairly steep angle. The end needs to be flat or slightly undercut so that the mallet can be stood on it when finished.

8 Refine the head and handle with the skew chisel, so that the handle has a slight taper to it. Stop the lathe occasionally and try the grip until it is comfortable. The head can be a little bulbous or can taper towards the handle, depending on your preference.

9 The meat tenderizer is made in exactly the same stages, but with a smaller diameter, and the head is flat rather than tapered. Divide the face with equidistant pencil lines—here, there are seven—which are the apexes of the grooves.

10 Begin to cut the "V" grooves between these lines with the skew chisel (Technique 12). Start the cuts with the long point of the chisel, arcing it into the cut rather than pushing it in.

11 You may find it easier to cut one side of each groove all the way along the face, so that the tool is not continually changing direction. Set the angle up on the first cut and treat each one the same, cutting to the same depth in each of the grooves.

12 Repeat this sequence of cuts in the opposite direction until all the grooves have equal depths and widths. If the grooves have been cut cleanly, they shouldn't need sanding; otherwise, sand them first and then the face to keep the crispness on the apexes.

13 Coat the workpiece with liquid paraffin and sand it with a piece of worn 320-grit sandpaper, then part it off and clean up the ends (see pages 74–75).

Door wedges

YOU WILL NEED

FOR TURNING
- Fingernail-ground spindle gouge
- Bandsaw
- Wood to match floors or furniture, i.e., pine, ash, oak, or cherry; dimensions 1½ x 1½ x 9 in (35 x 35 x 230 mm)
- Top speed of your lathe

In this project you get two items out of one piece by cutting the finished piece in half on a bandsaw. Extra care should be taken when finding and marking centers and mounting the blank because any discrepancy will show where the square shoulders meet the round.

TECHNIQUES FINDER	**2:** Using a bandsaw, pages 32–33
	5: Center finding, page 45
	6: Mounting between centers, pages 46–47
	11: Using a spindle gouge, pages 54–57

1 Mark the centers of the blank exactly (Technique 5) and mount it carefully on the lathe (Technique 6). Measure 2 in (50 mm) from each end and square off a pencil line on three faces, so that the line is visible when the wood is rotating.

2 When roughing out the ends with the spindle gouge, be careful not to cut past the line of the shoulders. Make sure that the diameter is smaller than the square section, so that when it is finished just the flat face rests on the floor.

3 Aim to cut the shoulders in one motion, rolling the tool through an arc, starting with the flute horizontal and finishing just about vertically (Technique 11).

4 Using only one tool saves time and builds up your skills. You can cut all the shapes needed with the same fingernail-ground gouge.

5 Hand-sand the workpiece, then part off, using the spindle gouge, and clean up the ends. No finish is necessary on the wedges, but you can apply one after cutting if preferred.

6 Mark a line using a straightedge diagonally from just under each shoulder on one of the flat faces, so that the end of each wedge is radiused after cutting. Using the bandsaw, cut along the line, not to one side (Technique 2); the saw marks can be left to provide extra grip or sanded off.

The wedges will never be used together at the same time, so the knobs can have different designs. This is an opportunity to put your own design ideas into practice.

Faceplate and spindle turning

This section covers projects that are a mixture of spindle work and faceplate turning. However, it is mainly concerned with pieces in which the workpiece is held by one end only, with the grain running parallel to the axis. In these projects, the blank starts off fixed between centers while it is roughed out to a cylinder before the spigot or spigots are created. These are then gripped by the jaws of the chuck while the piece is turned.

· ·

The primary advantage of combining techniques that use the two uses of the lathe is that it enables the woodturner to attempt more ambitious shapes and forms, which cannot be created using just the spindle or faceplate on its own. As you become more experienced, you will begin to discover your own style and almost certainly will find yourself producing more experimental pieces.

As with spindle turning, you will need to use a roughing gouge for the initial work, and then a parting tool and a skew chisel for further shaping, refinements, and decorations.

Scoop
By combining faceplate turning
and spindle turning techniques
you can develop you own style
and really experiment.

Faceplate and spindle-turning ideas
1 Kitchen towel holder
2 Chinese box
3 Flower
4 Round-bottomed box
5 Mushroom
6 Ringstand
7 Scoop
8 Spinning top
9 Caddy spoons

Mushroom

Mushrooms and toadstools, or gnome homes and fairy houses as they are otherwise known, are a bit of woodturning fun. There is no set pattern for them: they can be tall, short, fat, or thin. They are mostly made from branch wood to give them a natural edge.

YOU WILL NEED

FOR TURNING
• Spindle gouge
• Parting tool
• Split-free, dry branch wood, i.e., yew; dimensions 2½ in (65 mm) diameter x 6 in (150 mm) long
• Top speed of your lathe

FOR FINISHING
• Friction polish

TECHNIQUES FINDER	**6:** Mounting between centers, pages 46–47
	10: Parting, pages 52–53
	11: Using a spindle gouge, pages 54–57

1 Mount the blank between centers (Technique 6) and cut a spigot to suit your chuck.

2 Fit the chuck to the lathe and ensure that the blank is firmly gripped in the chuck (Technique 6).

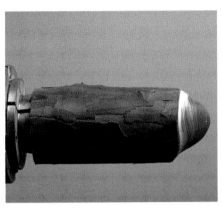

3 Cut the shape of the head with your spindle gouge (Technique 11). To create a gentle curve without any facets, start the cut and move the tool through to the center in one motion.

4 From time to time, stop the lathe, check that you are happy with the shape, and take another cut if necessary.

5 Carefully sand and polish the head (see pages 74–79). Start cutting under the head, taking care that the wings of the tool do not catch as you proceed with the cut.

6 This is what can happen when you are not watching the wings of the tool carefully enough.

7 If you do have a disaster, part the damaged head off and start again, this time without the dig-in. If you have trouble starting the cut because the tool skids away, use the parting tool to make an entry cut (Technique 10).

8 Shape the underside of the head and cut a stem which slightly tapers from the base and has a small radius where it joins the head. This makes it easier to sand, and doesn't look as though the head was stuck on afterwards.

9 Sand and polish the workpiece, making sure that you keep your fingers away from the natural edges (see pages 74–79 and 93).

10 Don't part off the workpiece totally with the parting tool, but leave a small stub to saw through and pare this away with a sharp knife or chisel.

Try to make each mushroom unique—
have you ever seen two identical ones?

Ring stand

This project is an ideal way to use up left-over offcuts that are too good to throw away. Plain woods can be decorated or colored to make them more attractive. A simple hand-bell shape works well, but this doesn't have to be adhered to. The stem should not be too ornate or too large in diameter, as this would make it difficult to place and remove the rings.

· ·

TECHNIQUES FINDER	**6:** Mounting between centers, pages 46–47 **7:** Mounting on a screw chuck, page 48 **10:** Parting, pages 52–53 **12:** Using a skew chisel, pages 58–61

1 Prepare and mount the blank firmly in the chuck (Techniques 6 and 7). Reduce about 1½ in (35 mm) of the length with the spindle gouge, leaving the diameter slightly larger than the final diameter.

2 Make a cut about ³/₁₆ in (5 mm) deep close to the chuck with the parting tool; this acts as a definition for the base and the largest diameter to work away from.

3 To develop the body, start the cuts slightly away from the base, moving along the body and over the shoulder in one cut (Technique 10).

4 Blend the shoulder into the stem to create a pleasing overall shape, but don't leave the stem too thick or it will look ungainly. When you are satisfied with the shape, sand the piece down to 240-grit sandpaper.

5 Decide where you want to put the decorative burn lines and mark them with a pencil. Use the long point of the skew chisel to lightly score each pencil line so that you can locate the line burner without it skating around (Technique 12).

6 Position the line-burning wire in a groove and stretch it slightly around the piece until the wire gets hot enough to burn in the line. Continue with the line burner in the rest of the grooves, keeping the decoration even.

7 The line-burning effect shouldn't be too overpowering and can only be used easily on nearly flat surfaces, where the wire can be pulled at right angles to the axis.

8 The workpiece only needs a final sanding with 320-grit sandpaper (see pages 74–79). You can then apply the friction polish and bring it to a glossy finish (see page 93).

9 When parting off, slightly angle the parting tool so that it undercuts the base (Technique 10).

Remember to make sure that the stand is level.

Spinning top

Making spinning tops is a lot of fun, and they keep children amused for ages. They can be enhanced with various forms of decoration: color, texture, simple grooves, and even paint. This type of top is spun between thumb and forefinger, and needs a slender spindle to generate the necessary speed.

YOU WILL NEED

FOR TURNING
- Skew chisel
- Spindle gouge
- Heavy, dense hardwood, i.e., lignum vitae, cocobolo, or partridge wood; dimensions $2^1/_2$ x $2^1/_2$ x $2^1/_2$ in (65 x 65 x 65 mm)
- Top speed of your lathe

FOR FINISHING
- Friction polish

TECHNIQUES FINDER	**7:** Mounting on a screw chuck, page 48 **11** Using a spindle gouge, pages 54–57 **12:** Using a skew chisel, pages 58–61

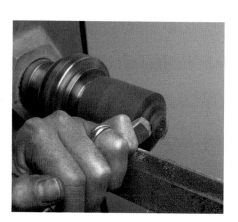

1 Prepare and mount the blank in the chuck (Technique 7). With the long point of the skew chisel, cut a shallow taper down to a fine point, like cutting one half of a "V." Try to make the final cut as clean and straight as possible, to minimize the amount of sanding needed.

2 Start to remove the waste with the spindle gouge, to give yourself enough space to work with the skew (Technique 11). The body should be about $^3/_4$ in (19 mm) long.

3 Refine the upper face with the skew chisel and decorate it with a series of small grooves, using the point (Technique 12). Sand and polish both faces at this stage, taking care not to round off the point (see pages 74–79 and 93).

4 The spindle should be about 1¹/₂ in (35 mm) long. To give it some strength, you can either flare it into the face or thicken it up with a decorative bead.

5 As you continue to make the stem thinner, you may need to support it with your left hand. Ideally, the finished stem should be about ³/₁₆ in (5 mm) in diameter.

6 As you part the top off with the long point of the skew chisel, try not to tear the fibers by gripping it too tightly.

The harder and heavier the wood you use, the longer the top will spin.

Kitchen towel holder

In this project the grain runs at 90° to the axis of the base, and parallel in the stem. For stability, the diameter of the base needs to be about a third of the overall height, and the stem needs to be thick enough to look in proportion, but not so thick that the kitchen roll can't fit or rotate freely.

· ·

YOU WILL NEED

FOR TURNING
- Roughing gouge
- Spindle gouge
- Bowl gouge
- Shear scraper
- Parting tool
- Skew chisel
- Sizing calipers
- Jacobs chuck
- 1 in (25 mm) sawtooth bit
- Wood glue
- Relatively heavy wood, i.e., beech, ash, oak, yew, or walnut; dimensions (base) 6¹/₂ x 1³/₄ in (165 x 45 mm)/ (stem) 1¹/₂ x 1¹/₂ x 12 in (40 x 40 x 290 mm)
- Medium to fast lathe speed for the base, and fast for the stem

FOR FINISHING
- Melamine or friction polish

1 Prepare the base blank (Technique 1) and mount it firmly on the screw chuck (Technique 7).

2 Position the tool rest so that it is parallel to the edge of the blank, and true up with the bowl gouge (Technique 13).

TECHNIQUES FINDER	**1:** Converting lumber, pages 28–31	**12:** Using a skew chisel, pages 58–61
	7: Mounting on a screw chuck, page 48	**13:** Using a bowl gouge, page 62
	9: Roughing, pages 50–51	**14:** Using a scraper, page 63
	10: Parting, pages 52–53	**15:** Drilling on the lathe, pages 64–65

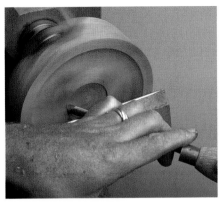

3 With the tool rest parallel to the face and at a height so that the tool edge is working on the center line, true up the base using your bowl gouge. This will ensure that the blank is as balanced as possible, allowing you to cut the chuck recess accurately.

4 Undercut the base to create a lip or foot about $^{3}/_{8}$ in (10 mm) wide and $^{3}/_{16}$ in (5 mm) deep. Using a pair of dividers, mark the size of the chuck recess in the center of this face and hollow it to a depth of $^{1}/_{8}$–$^{3}/_{16}$ in (3–4 mm).

5 The most accurate way to create the recess is to cut the dovetail with a fingernail gouge, but if you are not comfortable with this method, use the long point of a skew chisel (Technique 12).

6 The recess can be disguised by cutting some shallow beads with the fingernail gouge, making it look like a bit of extra decoration. Sand the whole face, taking care not to oversand the recess and obliterate the detail, then apply your preferred finish.

7 With the base mounted onto the scroll chuck, turn the edge using the bowl gouge to cut a concave curve which tapers into the upper face. A small step at either end adds definition to the ends of this curve.

8 Use the shear scraper on the face to remove any unevenness and to ensure that it is flat and ready to be sanded and polished (Technique 14).

9 Use a piece of tape to mark a 1 in (25 mm) depth mark on the shank of a sawtooth bit, then fit it in a Jacobs chuck and drill a hole in the center of the base (Technique 15).

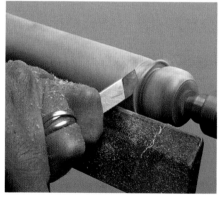

10 Mount the stem between centers and rough it down with a roughing gouge (Technique 9). Nearly all of the stem will be hidden by the kitchen roll, so it can be left fairly plain, with just the exposed section decorated. Here, a large bead was used, but an acorn would be a nice touch in oak.

11 Sand and polish before carefully measuring and cutting the socket with the calipers and parting tool (Technique 10). Very slightly undercut the shoulder that will be in contact with the upper face of the base, so when they are glued together there isn't an unsightly gap.

12 Check the fit before parting off, and adjust if necessary.

13 Glue the base and stem together with waterproof PVA glue or similar.

Scoop

From a tiny salt scoop to a large one for animal feeds, the method of turning varies little. The bowl is shaped like a goblet, with the opening slightly narrower than the body, rather than straight-sided, and with a handle in place of the stem.

· ·

YOU WILL NEED

FOR TURNING
- Fingernail-ground spindle gouge
- $\frac{1}{2}$ in (12 mm) drill bit
- Parting tool
- Scraper
- Hardwood, i.e., beech, sycamore, maple, or birch; dimensions $2\frac{3}{4}$ x $2\frac{3}{4}$ x 6 in (70 x 70 x 150 mm)
- Fast lathe speed

FOR FINISHING
- Liquid paraffin

TECHNIQUES FINDER	**7:** Mounting on a screw chuck, page 48
	11: Using a spindle gouge, pages 54–57
	12: Using a skew chisel, pages 58–61
	14: Using a scraper, page 63
	15: Drilling on the lathe, pages 64–65

1 Prepare and mount the blank in the chuck (Technique 7). Measure off $2\frac{1}{2}$ in (65 mm) on your spindle gouge or $\frac{1}{2}$ in (12 mm) drill held in a Jacobs chuck, and mark the depth with a piece of masking tape.

2 Line up the point of the gouge with the center of the blank and plunge it in, withdrawing the tool regularly to clear the shavings, until you reach the tape (Technique 15). Drilling this hole takes away any later uncertainty as to the depth of the bowl.

3 Start hollowing the bowl with a fingernail-ground spindle gouge laid on its side, making small cuts in an arc from the center outwards to the rim (Technique 11).

4 Open out and deepen the bowl, keeping the eventual goblet shape in mind as you proceed.

5 As you get deeper into the bowl you may need to use a scraper, which has a stiffer shank and will flex less while cutting (Technique 14).

6 Refine the internal shape, eliminating any ridges and hollows, and aim to leave a smooth, full curve.

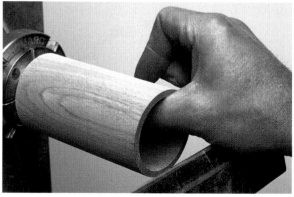

7 Stop the lathe occasionally and check the shape and depth of the bowl until you are happy with it. Touch gives you a far better representation of the shape than the eye can. When it feels right, sand the inside to as good a finish as you would on the outside (see pages 74–79).

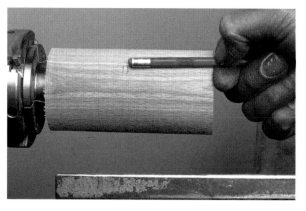

8 Measure the depth of the bowl and transfer it to the outside. Resist the temptation to add a bit, as this only makes it more difficult to keep track of the bowl's depth and therefore achieve an even wall thickness.

9 Part in at the headstock side of the first line to about two-thirds of the overall diameter or until the sound begins to change. Go too far, and you will end up with a miniature lampshade.

10 Shape the outside of the bowl to match the internal curve, using your spindle gouge and aiming for an eventual wall thickness of about $\frac{1}{8}$ in (3 mm).

11 Create a bead where the handle meets the bowl. If everything has gone as planned, this should be about the same diameter that you finished the parting cut (see Step 9).

12 The handle should be kept simple but still flowed through the bowl so that it doesn't look like an afterthought.

13 After sanding, round off the end of the handle so that it has a comfortable grip and part it off with the skew chisel (Technique 12). Hold the bowl loosely with your left hand to stop its hitting the tool rest as it comes free.

14 Pare away any waste, and hand-sand the end to remove any tooling marks (see pages 74–79).

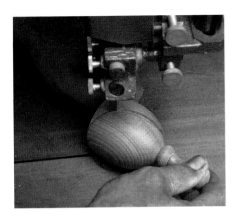

15 Cut away the waste on the bandsaw, pulling it through from behind the blade—be very careful with your fingers and thumbs.

16 Final shaping can be done on a belt sander or, as here, a drum sander mounted on the lathe. Hand-sand sharp edges left by the drum.

17 Give the scoop a coat of food-safe liquid paraffin (see page 95).

Round-bottomed box

This shallow box, with a smooth profile and close-fitting lid, is designed to fit into purses or pockets. Wood is affected by humidity and is constantly moving with changing conditions, so the box should be under 3 in (75 mm) diameter, otherwise the fit may be unpredictable.

YOU WILL NEED

FOR TURNING
- Roughing gouge
- Spindle gouge
- Parting tool
- Scraper
- Fine-grained, well-seasoned, dense hardwood, i.e., purpleheart; dimensions 2¹/₂ x 2¹/₂ x 2³/₄ in (65 x 65 x 70 mm)
- Fast lathe speed

FOR FINISHING
- Friction or melamine polish

TECHNIQUES FINDER	
6: Mounting between centers, pages 46–47	**14:** Using a scraper, page 63
7: Mounting on a screw chuck, page 48	
10: Parting, pages 52–53	
11: Using a spindle gouge, pages 54–57	

1 Mount the blank between centers (Technique 6), rough out a cylinder, and cut a spigot at both ends for your chuck.

2 Halfway along the blank, make a parting cut about ³/₁₆ in (5 mm) deep and wide enough to allow for a ³/₁₆-in (5-mm) wide spigot plus the width of your narrowest parting cut (Technique 10).

3 Use the narrow parting tool to part the free end of the blank. Try to leave a tiny shoulder on the face to make sizing the opening in the lid easier later on.

4 Hollow out the half of the blank left in the chuck into a concave curve, using the narrow scraper or side-ground spindle gouge (Technique 11). Leave a small, flat area on top of the spigot.

5 To get the best possible finish, use a round-nosed scraper to shear cut the inside, removing any high spots or torn grain (Technique 14).

6 Many woods don't like too much heat from excessive sanding, which is why you want to get the best possible finish using the tool. Gently sand and polish the interior and the spigot (see pages 74–79 and 93).

7 Remove the polished half and mount the other half in the chuck (Technique 7). Hollow it out in the same way as before, but this time create a shoulder for the spigot on the other half to fit into.

8 At this stage it needs to have a tight fit, tight enough to act as a jam chuck, but not so tight that you split the base by forcing it.

9 Remove the bulk of the waste and begin to develop the rounded shape, taking delicate cuts with a sharp spindle gouge.

10 Refine the shape so that it follows the inside until it flares out at the lips. You may need to check the wall thickness by taking it off the base. When you are satisfied with the shape, sand and polish this half, remove it from the base and carefully sand and then polish the inside of the half held in the chuck (see page 93).

11 On a scrap block or the end of the next prepared blank, cut a spigot to fit the base on for finishing.

12 Make the spigot so that the base will fit with just a gentle tap with the heel of your hand. Slightly dome all of these spigots, so that you are not trying to make two flat surfaces match up.

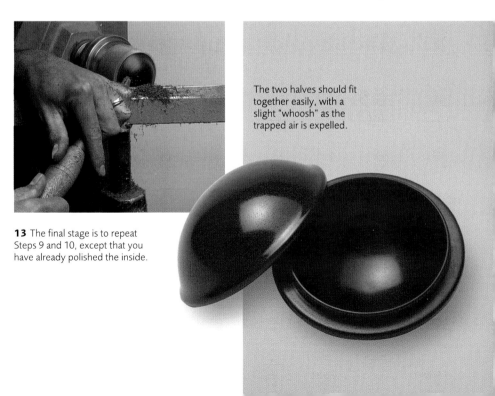

The two halves should fit together easily, with a slight "whoosh" as the trapped air is expelled.

13 The final stage is to repeat Steps 9 and 10, except that you have already polished the inside.

Faceplate turning

The term "faceplate turning" normally refers to the fact that the grain is rotating at 90° to its axis, which means that you have two areas of end grain to deal with. However, it also means that the object being turned is held only at one end—before the advent of woodturning chucks, everything that was to be held at one end was screwed onto a faceplate.

The spindle-turning rule of cutting from the largest diameter to the smallest becomes less of a dogma when you start faceplate turning; you have to think more of cutting with the grain so that the fibers being cut are supported by the fibers beneath them. Beginning turners are quite often lured into turning bowls and platters before they have fully acquired the skill with tools and the understanding of how and why they work that comes from spindle turning.

Gouges and scrapers are used for faceplate turning. The latter are generally heavier in section and have longer handles than spindle tools to cope with the greater forces that can be generated when the tools overhang the tool rest by a bigger margin than when turning between centers.

Create beautiful vessels like this end-grain hollow form by using gouges and scrapers, and working with the grain of the wood.

Faceplate-turning ideas
1 Simple bowl in fine, even-textured wood
2 End-grain hollow form in wet wood
3 Natural-edge bowl in laburnum

YOU WILL NEED

FOR TURNING
- Chuck
- Screw adapter
- $^3/_8$ in (10 mm) bowl gouge
- Calipers
- Shear scraper
- Drill and bit
- Skew chisel
- Fine, even-textured wood, i.e., sycamore, ripple sycamore, or beech; dimensions $2^1/_2$ x 5 in (60 x 125 mm)
- Medium to fast lathe speed

FOR FINISHING
- Danish oil

Simple bowl

Turning a bowl is one of the chief attractions of woodturning, creating a functional and aesthetically pleasing object. This project shows you how to turn a shallow bowl; you can become more adventurous as your skills and techniques improve.

TECHNIQUES FINDER	**7:** Mounting on a screw chuck, page 48 **12:** Using a skew chisel, pages 58–61 **13:** Using a bowl gouge, page 62 **14:** Using a scraper, page 63

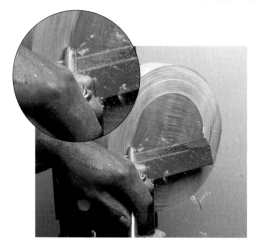

1 Prepare the blank and mount it on the screw chuck (Technique 7). True up the face and edge with your bowl gouge so that the blank is as balanced as possible.

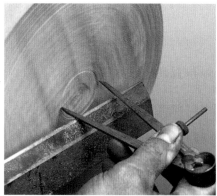

2 Mark the diameter of the chuck recess with the left-hand point of the calipers. Be careful not to allow the right-hand point to come in contact with the wood.

3 Start cutting the recess with your bowl gouge (Technique 13). At this stage, it only needs to be a shallow indentation of around $1/8$ in (3 mm).

4 Use the long point of the skew chisel to cut the dovetail for the jaws to expand into (Technique 12). The recess can be decorated with a series of beads.

5 Start the cuts at the edge of the blank, working from the smallest diameter to the largest. The flute should always point in the direction that you want to make the cut, and the bevel should always be in contact with the wood.

6 Try to make each cut one fluid motion from start to finish, so that you get a smooth curve rather than a multi-faceted surface. Note how the shavings are coming off the lower portion of the cutting edge and the bevel is supporting the cut.

7 Start each cut by rubbing the bevel first, then raise the handle until shavings begin to appear, and then advance the cut around the curve in one motion.

8 Watch the depth of cut (the amount of wood being removed), and try to keep this constant by moving the handle in a smooth arc as you follow the curve.

9 Note how the tool changes position from the one in Step 7, through Step 8, and into the finish of the cut here in one motion, remaining in contact with the surface throughout.

10 The surface and curve can be refined by shear scraping. The edge of the scraper is angled at about 45° and drawn across the surface, allowing the fine burr to work (Technique 14).

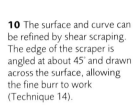

11 This method is especially effective on end grain, as the ends of the fibers are sliced off by the shearing action.

12 The surface can then be sanded by hand or power sanded, working your way up from 120 grit, through 150, 180, and 240, and finishing off with 320 grit (see pages 74–79).

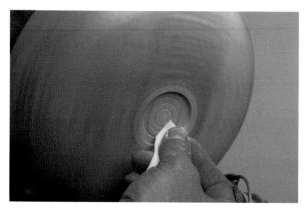

13 To get into the detail of the recess effectively, use small, folded strips of abrasive.

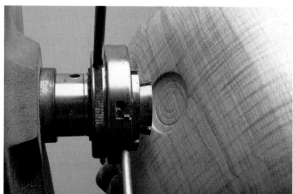

14 Make sure that the jaws of the chuck and the recess are clean, so that the bowl runs true after mounting. Don't overtighten the chuck, as this could cause the blank to run out of true.

15 On the inside of a bowl the cuts are made from the largest diameter to the smallest. This is the opposite to the outside, but the same thing is happening—each fiber is being supported by the ones behind or below it.

16 There is nowhere to rub the bevel at the start of each cut, so the tool must be held so that the bevel is parallel to the cut to be made, with the flute pointing in the direction of the cut. In this way, as soon as the cut is started, the bevel will begin to rub and support the cut.

17 As with the outside of the bowl, the way the gouge is controlled governs how the shape is achieved. At the start of the cut, the tool is angled across the face of the bowl.

18 Keep the depth of the cut constant by sweeping the handle in an arc. With a tool as long as the bowl gouge, the amount of movement at the handle end directly relates to the amount of movement at the cutting edge.

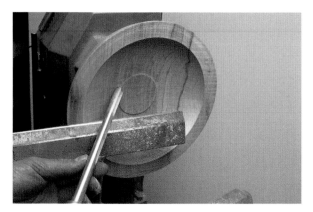

19 As the cut finishes, the tool is angled away from the bowl, but the bevel is still in contact with the surface. The whole cut should be accomplished in one sweep of the gouge.

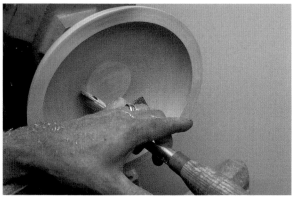

20 Shear-scrape the interior surface to remove any irregularities, working from the rim into the center.

21 Sand the rim and interior with the same series of grits as the outside, eliminating any torn end grain with the coarsest grit before moving to the next grit.

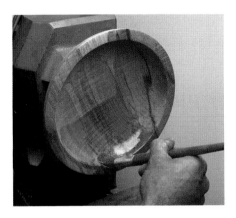

22 With the lathe stationary, liberally brush a coat of oil over the whole piece. Leave it for a few minutes to penetrate, then wipe off the surplus with kitchen towels. Burnish the surface by holding the towel against it while the lathe is running (see pages 93–97).

23 The final touch is to write the name of the wood, your name, and the date in the recess with a fine indelible marker.

24 Apply several coats of oil, leaving drying intervals, to achieve a durable finish.

Natural-edge bowl

This bowl uses the natural shape of the outside of the log; sometimes the bark can be incorporated into the design. If turned in wet woods, these bowls need to be thin-walled to allow for distortion without splitting or cracking as they dry.

• •

YOU WILL NEED

FOR TURNING
• Chuck
• Bowl gouge
• Shear scraper
• Bowl calipers
• Dividers
• Carver's gouge
• Wet or dry wood, i.e., laburnum (used here); dimensions $4\frac{1}{2}$ in (115 mm) deep x $7\frac{1}{2}$ in (190 mm) in diameter
• Slow to medium lathe speed

FOR FINISHING
• Danish oil
• Fine paste wax

TECHNIQUES FINDER	
2: Using a bandsaw, pages 32–33	**14:** Using a scraper, page 63
3: Sharpening, pages 34–43	
7: Mounting on a screw chuck, page 48	
13: Using a bowl gouge, page 62	

1 Cut the blank to the required size on the bandsaw (Technique 2), and mount it between centers with the natural edge facing the headstock. At this stage you need to align the piece to get the top edges as balanced as possible in the finished bowl.

2 With the lathe speed set quite slow, begin removing the waste (Technique 13). Because the grain is oriented at 90° to its axis, you need to start the cuts from the tailstock and work toward the headstock.

3 As the blank gets more balanced, increase the lathe speed—this speeds up the waste removal and makes it easier to get the gouge to flow round the shape. Don't get too carried away with making shavings and forget the foot or spigot that will be gripped in the chuck.

4 Set the measuring calipers to the appropriate size for your chuck to grip in contraction mode, and transfer this to the blank. Carefully cut the spigot with the point of the gouge, creating a dovetail if necessary. The foot needs to have a small flat area at the circumference; the area within is then domed and the pimple under the tailstock is carved off and sanded just before it is mounted in the chuck.

5 It is always a good idea to resharpen your gouge before making your final cuts (Technique 3). This should minimize tearout on the end grain and reduce the amount of sanding needed.

6 Use the shear scraper to refine the shape and remove any ridges. Angle the tool to about 45° and draw it around the profile, letting the fine burr do the work (Technique 14). By angling the tool edge, the fibers are sliced, rather than dragged off.

7 The finish achieved with the shear scraper may uncover fine cracks that were not noticeable before. Repair these by running a medium-viscosity superglue into them, using the capillary tubing supplied. When the glue is dry, use the shear scraper to remove the excess.

8 The safest way to sand natural-edged bowls is with a 3 in (75 mm) power sanding arbor mounted in an electric drill. Hold the sander lightly against the surface; don't apply too much pressure on the arbor, as this only generates excessive heat, causing small cracks to appear (see pages 74–79).

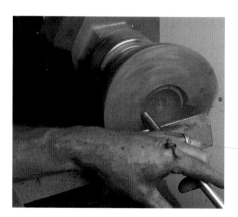

9 Remove the tailstock nipple with a shallow carver's gouge, and then sand. Mount the bowl in the chuck and make sure that it is secure (Technique 7), but don't overtighten the chuck to the extent that it crushes the foot and causes a weakness between the bowl and foot. Start hollowing out the bowl.

10 Work out toward the rim, cutting only deep enough to clear the uneven rim. A lot of the time the gouge will be cutting air, especially as you start each cut, so it is important to ensure that the bevel is parallel with the cut face each time you make an entry cut.

11 It is important that you establish the required wall thickness at this stage, particularly if you are turning wet wood. If you try to work the whole face in one go when it is very thin, you could shatter the piece.

12 Check the wall thickness regularly, with double-ended calipers if you have them, or feel the wall between your finger and thumb.

13 Be careful not to catch the edge of the sander on the rim, but at the same time keep the sanding face as flat as possible to the surface so that you don't round off the edges.

14 Paint the oil on with a brush, working it into all the nooks and crannies in the natural edges. Leave for a few minutes and wipe off the excess with kitchen towel. If several coats are needed, these can be done off the lathe.

15 When the oil has dried, apply a coat of fine paste wax (see page 97).

End-grain hollow form

This project shows how to turn a hollow form in wet wood so that it doesn't split. When turning wet wood, ribbons stream off the tools, which need sharpening less often. If the project cannot be finished in one session, wrap plastic around it to stop it drying out.

YOU WILL NEED

FOR TURNING
- Sideground bowl gouge
- Shear scraper
- Mighty Midget hollowing tool
- Cobra head
- Scroll chuck with large jaws, or faceplate ring
- Wall-thickness calipers
- Fine-toothed saw
- Wastewood cone
- Shallow fluted carving gouge
- Even-grained pale woods, i.e., maple, sycamore, silver birch, basswood, or European ripple sycamore; dimensions 12 in (300 mm) long x 9 in (230 mm) in diameter; if using a faceplate ring, allow about 2 in (50 mm) extra length for the screws
- Slow to medium lathe speed

FOR FINISHING
- Danish oil or automotive clear cellulose lacquer

1 Use a circular disc to find the center and mark the rough diameter, then mount the piece between centers after deciding which end is to be the top of the form (Technique 6).

2 Rough out the block to a cylinder and square up the ends, particularly the end that is mounted into the chuck, which needs to be slightly concave right up to the live center.

TECHNIQUES FINDER	**6:** Mounting between centers, pages 46–47	**15:** Drilling on the lathe, pages 64–65
	7: Mounting on a screw chuck, page 48	**18:** Hollowing, pages 70–71
	13: Using a bowl gouge, page 62	
	14: Using a scraper, page 63	

3 Measure and mark the diameter of the spigot for the chuck or faceplate ring, and start to remove the waste from around the base. Tuck the tool handle into your hip and move your body with the gouge so that you are using mass rather than muscle (Technique 13).

4 Move to the other end of the blank and cut away the waste from this end, keeping in mind the required shape, using a sideground gouge that sprays the shavings away from you.

5 Turn the piece roughly to shape. Having the base at the tailstock end allows you better access to the spigot area, and if you are right-handed you will find it easier to make the cuts in this direction, where the majority of the waste is removed.

6 Carefully cut the dovetail spigot to suit the chuck jaws, ensuring that the angle of the dovetail matches that of the jaws. If you are using a small faceplate or faceplate ring, turn the spigot down to their outside diameter. Leave the tail center mark.

7 Mount the blank in the chuck or onto the plate or ring, and bring up the tailstock for added stability (Technique 7). When you restart the lathe, the piece will probably not run true. Leave some bulk at the base to provide strength while hollowing.

8 Develop the shape with the gouge, then use the shear scraper to refine it. A shear scraper is a lot easier to control, as it removes far less than a cutting tool, and if kept sharp it will produce a very fine finish (Technique 14).

9 With the lathe set at a slow speed, drill a hole down the center (Technique 15). A $^7/_8$ in (22 mm) sawtooth bit, mounted in a boring bar, was used here after the internal depth was set by measuring on the outside and marking the bit with tape.

10 Using a Mighty Midget hollowing tool, make cuts from the center outward to a depth about level with the widest point of the vessel, or about two-fifths of the internal depth (Technique 18).

11 Open out this section of the vessel, removing the waste, until you have the required even wall thickness of about ⅛ in (3 mm). Depending on the shape of your vessel, you may need to use the cobra head to cut in under the shoulder.

12 The amount of light transmitted through the wet wood by a lamp shone on the outside of the vessel will give you a good guide to the wall thickness.

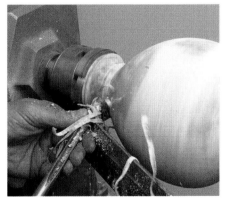

13 It is safest to use a pair of calipers set a bit wider than the required wall thickness to get a truly accurate reading of the vessel wall.

14 Continue hollowing and finishing the walls in stages, then reduce the bulk left earlier around the base, following the outside curve past the point which will eventually become the foot.

15 The finish from the shear scraper should need a minimum of sanding: you should be able to start at 180 grit, proceeding through to 320 grit. Power sanding with an electric drill produces the best results (see pages 74–79).

16 Unless you have a lathe that reverses, a certain number of fibers will have been laid over, like the nap of the cloth on a snooker table. Remove the fibers by hand-sanding along the grain with 600 grit.

17 Apply several coats of your chosen finish. Automotive cellulose lacquer was used here, because it dries very quickly (see page 96).

18 The interior of a vessel like this can be painted with black emulsion paint. This gives the opening definition and adds an air of mystery to the piece.

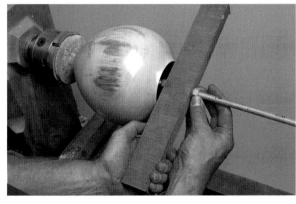

19 To ensure that the piece will not split, the base needs to be the same thickness as the walls. Determine the internal depth with a gauge made from a length of 2 x 4 that passes through a wooden crosspiece and is locked off at the exact depth with nuts on either side.

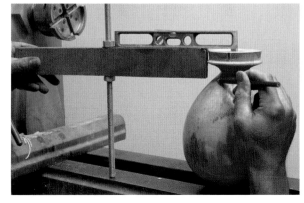

20 Remove the vessel from the chuck and invert it on a flat surface, then transfer the internal depth to the outside with a soft pencil or non-permanent felt-tip pen.

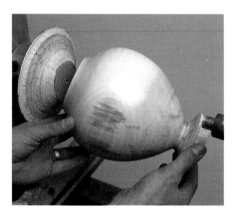

21 Use a scrap wood cone, mounted on the screw point with a protective nonslip surface, such as masking tape, to remount the vessel between centers so that the chuck spigot can be removed and a recessed foot created (see pages 80–83).

22 The reason for leaving the original tail center stub now becomes obvious as the vessel is remounted. Apply only enough pressure with the tailstock for the piece to be driven; any more and you will risk crushing it.

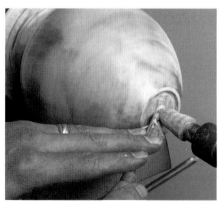

23 Remove the bulk of the spigot with a freshly sharpened bowl gouge, taking fine cuts down to the central stub. If you try to hurry, the piece will stall on the friction cone.

24 The base needs to be recessed so that, when totally dry, any unevenness can be sanded flat. Add the wall thickness and the depth of the recess to the pencil line—$1/8$ in (3 mm) for the wall thickness and $1/8$–$3/16$ in (3–4 mm) for the recess—and use a small detail gouge to make the cuts.

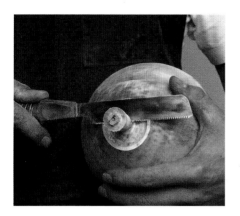

25 Carefully cut the waste stub off close to the base with a fine-toothed saw.

26 Pare away the rest of the stub with a shallow-fluted carving gouge, then hand-sand to remove any marks.

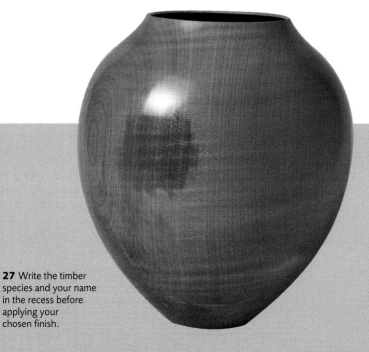

27 Write the timber species and your name in the recess before applying your chosen finish.

Gallery

Other people's work is a wonderful source of inspiration and reference. It can help you discover the sort of turning you are likely to enjoy, give you insights into the many different techniques you can use, and help spark your own design ideas.

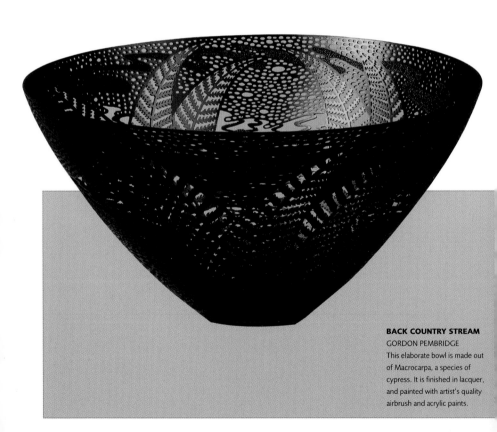

BACK COUNTRY STREAM
GORDON PEMBRIDGE
This elaborate bowl is made out of Macrocarpa, a species of cypress. It is finished in lacquer, and painted with artist's quality airbrush and acrylic paints.

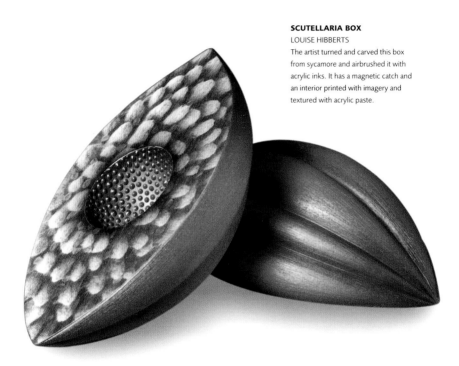

SCUTELLARIA BOX
LOUISE HIBBERTS
The artist turned and carved this box from sycamore and airbrushed it with acrylic inks. It has a magnetic catch and an interior printed with imagery and textured with acrylic paste.

BACK COUNTRY STREAM (DETAIL)
GORDON PEMBRIDGE
Here we can see the intricate pattern, and interplay of light and color, on Gordon Pembridge's bowl in detail.

SCUTELLARIA BOX (DETAIL)
LOUISE HIBBERTS
Here we can see how the airbrushing has given the exterior of the box a smooth, decorative finish.

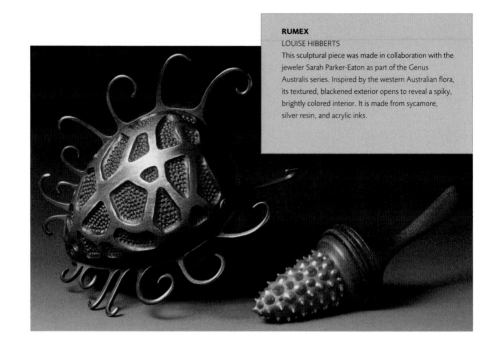

RUMEX
LOUISE HIBBERTS
This sculptural piece was made in collaboration with the jeweler Sarah Parker-Eaton as part of the Genus Australis series. Inspired by the western Australian flora, its textured, blackened exterior opens to reveal a spiky, brightly colored interior. It is made from sycamore, silver resin, and acrylic inks.

UMAMI BOWL
KERRY DEANE
This is a burl bowl, turned from arbutus wood. It was made by trimming rounded outgrowths from trees and hollowing them until smooth.

RED AND BLACK MILLS

LOUISE HIBBERTS

This salt and pepper mill set has been turned and carved from sycamore. The mills are airbrushed with acrylic inks and then textured with pigmented acrylic resin.

CROCHET HOOKS
WILLIAM SCHMIDT
This set of crochet hooks in various woods reflects
the years William has spent evolving his delicate
style of spindle turning. They also demostrate the
artistry once common in tool making.

REDWOOD BOWL
BARRY UDEN
This redwood burl bowl has
been finished with Waterlox
and wax, and buffed for a
beautiful and easily
maintained finish.

AMBOYNA AND COCOBOLO BOX
BARRY UDEN

This decorative box is made out of Amboyna Burl from narra timber, a wavy-grained wood with a swirling pattern, and cocobolo, a reddish-brown tropical hardwood. It was then buffed with carnuba wax for a glossy finish.

BURR OAK POD
ANGUS CLYNE

Hard, strong red oak was used to make this pod, which creates fascinating patterns of light and shadow as it rotates.

TWISTED STEM GOBLET
WES JONES
This goblet is made from African
blackwood and American holly.

TEAR DROP PEPPER MILLS
DENNIS CLOUTIER
Made out of big leaf maple, this innovative exploration
of shapes and materials turns these everyday objects
into works of art.

CANDLESTICKS

RUDE OSOLNIK

The wonderful forms and proportions of
these walnut candlesticks show how
simple design can have a rare elegance.

HOLLOW FORMS

PHIL IRONS

The carved embellishment and color of
these thin-walled, hollow forms unite them
as a collection.

RIPPLE MAPLE PLATTER
BARRY UDEN

The artist made this platter out of ripple maple, also known as flame maple. The outer edge was dyed green and it was buffed with carnuba wax.

ROCKING CHAIR
RAY JONES

One of the few remaining production turners, Ray drew on 40 years of turning experience to create this elegant rocking chair in spalted and rippled sycamore.

MAPLE VASE
MICHAEL JONES
The bark rim and the satin lacquer finish
create an interesting contrast of textures
on this vase, in spalted, soft maple burl.

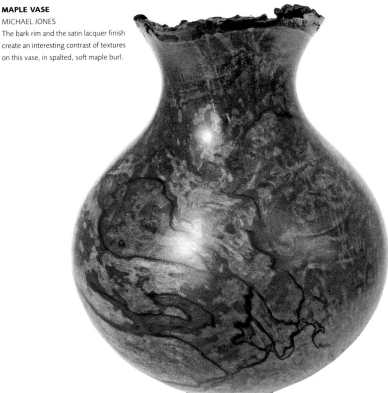

FISHY FRENZY IV
WES JONES
This bowl is made from tulip poplar,
a hardwood. Again, it is decorated
with pyrography, as well as delicate,
painted fish.

"INTERCONNECTIONS"
WES JONES
Wes Jones made this multi-cavity, hollow
form out of sugar maple. He then
decorated it using pyrography—scorching
designs into the wood.

CHERRY BOWL
JERRY SMITH
This beautiful cherry burl bowl was turned with a natural edge and is speckled
throughout. The irregular edge follows the natural contour of the wood, and the light
sap wood and reddish brown heartwood make a great combination.

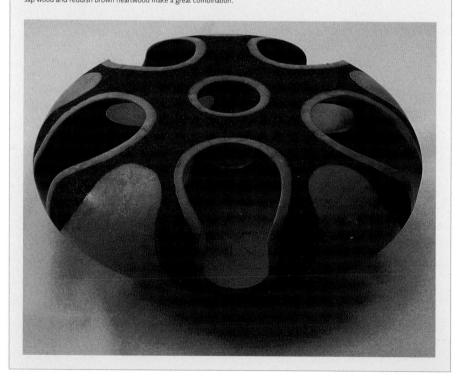

PEPPER MILL
DENNIS CLOUTIER
The clean lines and sleek design of this big leaf maple burl pepper mill highlight the grain of the wood and the precision of the turning.

COLORED VASE
SANDRA ADAMS
The inspiration for this ash vase came from observing waves breaking on a summer's day. The color has been achieved by mixing water-based dyes.

Index

Acknowledgements

Quarto would like to thank all the woodturners who contributed work for inclusion in this book. All other pictures are the copyright of Quarto Publishing, unless otherwise stated in the captions.

The measurements given in this book are only a guide—adapt them to suit your wood and needs. Measurements are given in imperial and metric (shown in brackets). When making a project, follow either the imperial or metric, but do not interchange them, since the equivalents are only approximate.

Phil Irons is a self-taught woodturner who turned professional in 1994. He teaches and demonstrates, mainly in his speciality of thin-walled, hollow forms, for which he has won numerous prizes. His work is in private and corporate collections throughout the world. More of his work can be seen on www.philirons.co.uk.